Evidence-Based Instruction in Reading

Fluency

Evidence-Based Instruction in Reading

A Professional Development Guide to Fluency

Nancy D. Padak
Kent State University

Timothy V. Rasinski
Kent State University

PEARSON

Boston • New York • San Francisco
Mexico City • Montreal • Toronto • London • Madrid • Munich • Paris
Hong Kong • Singapore • Tokyo • Cape Town • Sydney

Executive Editor: *Aurora Martínez Ramos*
Series Editorial Assistant: *Lynda Giles*
Marketing Manager: *Danae April*
Production Editor: *Gregory Erb*
Editorial Production Service: *Publishers' Design and Production Services, Inc.*
Composition Buyer: *Linda Cox*
Manufacturing Buyer: *Linda Morris*
Electronic Composition: *Publishers' Design and Production Services, Inc.*
Photo Researcher: *Naomi Rudov*
Cover Designer: *Kristina Mose-Libon*

For related titles and support materials, visit our online catalog at www.ablongman.com.

Between the time website information is gathered and then published, it is not unusual for some sites to have closed. Also, the transcription of URLs can result in typographical errors. The publisher would appreciate notification where these errors occur so that they may be corrected in subsequent editions.

Cataloging-in-Publication data unavailable at press time.

ISBN-10: 0-205-45629-4
ISBN-13: 978-0-205-45629-1

Printed in the United States of America

10 9 8 7 6 5 4 3 2 1   RRD-VA   11 10 09 08 07

Photo Credits: Pages 1, 13: T. Lindfors/Lindfors Photography; p. 27: Jeffry Myers/ IndexOpen; p. 39: VStock/IndexOpen; p. 53: Andrew M. Levine/Photo Researchers.

Among us, we have been teachers and teacher educators for nearly 100 years! During this time, we have developed deep and abiding respect for teachers and trust in their ability to offer their students the very best possible instruction. Yet we also agree with librarian John Cotton Dana (1856–1929), who said, "Who dares to teach must never cease to learn."

Our careers have been marked by continual learning. We dedicate this book to all who have taught us and all whom we have taught—all who have dared to teach.

NP
TR
MM
EN
BZ

Contents

CHAPTER 1

Fluency: What Does Research Tell Us?   1

CHAPTER 2

Instructional Strategies for Fluency Development   13

Series Introduction

Evidence-Based Instruction in Reading: A Professional Development Guide

Better than a thousand days of diligent study is one day spent with a great teacher.

JAPANESE PROVERB

*L*earning to read is perhaps a young child's greatest school accomplishment. Of course, reading is the foundation for success in all other school subjects. Reading is critical to a person's own intellectual development, later economic success, and the pleasure that is to be found in life.

Similarly, teaching a child to read is one of the greatest accomplishments a teacher can ever hope for. And yet, reading and teaching reading are incredibly complex activities. The reading process involves elements of a person's psychological, physical, linguistic, cognitive, emotional, and social world. Teaching reading, of course, involves all these and more. Teachers must orchestrate the individuality of each child they encounter; the physical layout of the classroom and attendant materials; their own colleagues, parents, and school administration; the school's specified curriculum; and their own style of teaching! The popular cliché that "reading is not rocket science" perhaps underestimates the enormity of the task of teaching children to read.

The complexity of teaching reading can be, quite simply, overwhelming. How does a teacher teach and find mastery of the various skills in reading, attending to the school and state curricular guidelines, using an appropriate variety of materials, while simultaneously meeting the individual needs of all children in the classroom? Because of this complexity, many schools and districts select reading programs xii

SERIES
INTRODUCTION
*Evidenced-Based
Instruction in
Reading*

to provide the structure and sequence for a given grade level. Following basal reading programs, for example, assures coverage of at least some key skills and content for reading. But no single program can be sensitive to the culture of the classroom, school, and community, the individual children in the classroom, and the instructional style of the teacher. Addressing these issues is the teacher's responsibility.

Despite everyone's best intentions, many children have failed to learn to read up to expectations. The results of periodic assessments of U.S. students' reading achievement, most notably the National Assessment of Educational Progress, have demonstrated little, if any, growth in student reading achievement over the past 30 years. This lack of growth in literacy achievement is at least partially responsible for equally dismal results in student growth in other subject areas that depend highly on a student's ability to read.

The National Reading Panel Report

Having noticed this disturbing trend, the National Reading Panel (NRP) was formed by the United States Congress in 1996 and given the mandate of reviewing the scientific research related to reading and determining those areas that science has shown have the greatest promise for improving reading achievement in the elementary grades. In 2000, the NRP came out with its findings. Essentially, the panel found that the existing scientific research points to five particular areas of reading that have the greatest promise of increasing reading achievement: phonemic awareness, phonics and word decoding, reading fluency, vocabulary, and reading comprehension. Additionally, the NRP indicated that investments in teachers, through professional development activities, hold promise of improving student reading achievement.

The findings of the NRP have been the source of considerable controversy, yet they have been used by the federal and state governments, as well as local school systems, to define and mandate reading instruction. In particular, the federal Reading First program has mandated that any school receiving funds from Reading First must embed within its reading curriculum direct and systematic teaching of phonemic awareness, phonics, reading fluency, vocabulary, and comprehension. The intent of the mandate, of course, is to provide students with the instruction that is based on best evidence that it will have a positive impact on students' reading achievement.

Although we may argue about certain aspects of the findings of the National Reading Panel, in particular what it left out of its report of effective instructional principles, we find ourselves in solid agreement with the panel that the five elements that it identified are indeed critical to success in learning to read.

Phonemic awareness is crucial to early reading development. Students must develop an ability to think about the sounds of language and to manipulate those sounds in various ways—to blend sounds, to segment words into sounds, and so on. An inability to deal with language sounds in this way will set the stage for difficulty in phonics and word decoding. To sound out a word, which is essentially what phonics requires of students, readers must have adequate phonemic awareness. Yet, some estimates indicate that as many as 20 percent of young children in the United States do not have sufficient phonemic awareness to profit fully from phonics instruction.

Phonics, or the ability to decode written words in text, is clearly essential for reading. Students who are unable to accurately decode at least 90 percent of the words they encounter while reading will have difficulty gaining appropriate meaning from what they read. We prefer to expand the notion of phonics to word decoding. Phonics, or using the sound–symbol relationship between letters and words is, without doubt, an important way to solve unknown words. However, there are other methods to decode written words. These include attending to the prefixes, suffixes, and base elements of longer words; examining words for rimes (word families) and other letter patterns; using meaningful context to determine unknown words; dividing longer words into smaller parts through syllabication; and making words part of one's sight vocabulary, words recognized instantly and by sight. Good readers are able to employ all of these strategies and more. Appropriately, instruction needs to be aimed at helping students develop proficiency in learning to decode words using multiple strategies.

Reading fluency refers to the ability to read words quickly, as well as accurately, and with appropriate phrasing and expression. Fluent readers are able to decode words so effortlessly that they can direct their cognitive resources away from the low-level decoding task to the more important meaning-making or comprehension part of reading. For a long time, fluency was a relatively neglected area of the reading curriculum. In recent years, however, educators have come to realize that although fluency deals with the ability to efficiently and effortlessly decode words, it is critical to good reading comprehension and needs to be part of any effective reading curriculum.

Word and concept meaning is the realm of *vocabulary*. Not only must readers be able to decode or sound out words but they must also

xiii

SERIES
INTRODUCTION
*Evidenced-Based
Instruction in
Reading*

xiv

SERIES
INTRODUCTION

*Evidenced-Based
Instruction in
Reading*

know what these words mean. Instruction aimed at expanding students' repertoire of word meanings and deepening their understanding of already known words is essential to reading success. Thus, vocabulary instruction is an integral part of an effective instructional program in reading.

Accurate and fluent decoding of words, coupled with knowledge of word meanings, may seem to ensure *comprehension.* However, there is more to it than that. Good readers also actively engage in constructing meaning, beyond individual words, from what they read. That is, they engage in meaning-constructing strategies while they read. These include ensuring that readers employ their background knowledge for the topics they encounter in reading. It also means that they ask questions, make predictions, and create mental images while they read. Additionally, readers monitor their reading comprehension and know when to stop and check things out when things begin to go awry—that is, when readers become aware that they are not making adequate sense out of what they are reading. These are just some of the comprehension strategies and processes good readers use while they read to ensure that they understand written texts. These same strategies must be introduced and taught to students in an effective reading instruction program.

Phonemic awareness, phonics/decoding, reading fluency, vocabulary, and comprehension are the five essential elements of effective reading programs identified by the National Reading Panel. We strongly agree with the findings of the NRP—these elements must be taught to students in their reading program.

Rather than get into in-depth detail on research and theory related to these topics, our intent in this series is to provide you with a collection of simple, practical, and relatively easy-to-implement instructional strategies, proven through research and actual practice, for teaching each of the five essential components. We think you will find the books in this series readable and practical. Our hope is that you will use these books as a set of handbooks for developing more effective and engaging reading instruction for all your students.

Professional Development in Literacy

Effective literacy instruction requires teachers to be knowledgeable, informed professionals capable of assessing student needs and responding to those needs with an assortment of instructional strategies. Whether you are new to the field or a classroom veteran, ongoing professional development is imperative. Professional development influences instructional practices which, in turn, affect student achievement (Wenglinsky, 2000). Effective professional development is not simply an isolated program or activity; rather it is an ongoing, consistent learning effort where links between theoretical knowledge and the application of that knowledge to daily classroom practices are forged in consistent and meaningful ways (Renyi, 1998).

Researchers have noted several characteristics of effective professional development: It must be grounded in research-based practices; it must be collaborative, allowing teachers ample opportunities to share knowledge, as well as teaching and learning challenges, among colleagues; and it must actively engage teachers in assessing, observing, and responding to the learning and development of their students (Darling-Hammond & McLaughlin, 1995). This professional development series, *Evidence-Based Instruction in Reading: A Professional Development Guide* is intended to provide a roadmap for systematic, participatory professional development initiatives.

Using the Books

The *Evidence-Based Instruction in Reading* series consists of five professional development books, each addressing one major component of literacy instruction identified by the National Reading Panel and widely accepted in the field as necessary for effective literacy programs: phonemic awareness, phonics, vocabulary, fluency, and comprehension. These five components are not, by any means, the only components needed for effective literacy instruction. Access to appropriate reading materials, productive home–school connections, and a desire to learn to read and write are also critical pieces of the literacy puzzle. It is our hope, however, that by focusing in depth on each of the five major literacy components, we can provide educators and professional development facilitators with concrete guidelines and suggestions for enhancing literacy instruction. Our hope is that teachers who read, reflect, and act on the information in these books will be more able to provide effective instruction in each of the five essential areas of reading.

Each book is intended to be used by professional development facilitators, be they administrators, literacy coaches, reading specialists, and/or classroom teachers, and program participants as they engage in professional development initiatives or in-service programs

xvi
....

SERIES
INTRODUCTION

*Evidenced-Based
Instruction in
Reading*

within schools or school districts. The use of the series can be adapted to meet the specific needs and goals of a group of educators. For example, a school may choose to hold a series of professional development sessions on each of the five major components of literacy instruction; it may choose to focus in depth on one or two components that are most relevant to its literacy program; or it may choose to focus on specific aspects, such as assessment or instructional strategies, of one or more of the five areas.

The books may also be useful in professional book club settings. An icon, included at spots for book club discussion, mark times when you might wish to share decisions about your own classroom to get colleagues' feedback. You might also want to discuss issues or solve problems with colleagues. Appendix C lists several other possible book club activities. These are listed by chapter and offer opportunities to delve into issues mentioned in the chapters in greater depth. It is important that, in collaboration with teachers, professional development needs be carefully assessed so that the appropriate content can be selected to meet those needs.

Overview of Book Content

To begin each book in the series, Chapter 1 presents a literature review that defines the literacy component to be addressed in that book, explains why this component is important in the context of a complete and balanced literacy program, and synthesizes key research findings that underlie the recommendations for evidence-based instructional practices that follow in subsequent chapters. The conclusion of Chapter 1 invites professional development program participants to analyze, clarify, extend, and discuss the material presented in this chapter.

Chapter 2 outlines general principles for instruction. Participants are asked to evaluate their own instructional practices and to plan for refinement of those practices based on their students' needs. Each suggested instructional strategy in this chapter is based on the research presented in Chapter 1 and includes the purpose, necessary materials, and procedures for implementation. Ideas for engaging professional development participants in extended discussions related to phonemic awareness, phonics, vocabulary, fluency, or comprehension are offered at the end of Chapter 2.

Chapter 3 begins by presenting broad themes for effective assessment such as focusing on critical information, looking for patterns of behavior, recognizing developmental progressions, deciding how much assessment information is needed, using instructional situations for assessment purposes, using assessment information to guide instruction, and sharing assessment information with children and families. At the end of Chapter 3, professional development participants are asked to evaluate their current assessment practices, draw conclusions about needed change, and develop plans for change. The conclusion of the chapter provides vignettes and questions designed to generate collaborative discussion about and concrete ways to enhance connections between assessment and classroom instruction.

Chapter 4 invites participants to think beyond classroom-based strategies by examining activities that can be recommended to families to support children's development of phonemic awareness, phonics, vocabulary, fluency, and comprehension at home. The final chapter provides a variety of print- and Web-based resources to support instruction in phonemic awareness, phonics, vocabulary, fluency, or comprehension.

Together, the information and activities included in these books, whether used as is or selectively, will foster careful consideration of research-based practice. Professional development participants will learn about the research that supports their current practices and will be guided to identify areas for improvement in their classroom programs.

The need for new programs and methods for teaching reading is questionable. What is without question is the need for great teachers of reading—teachers who are effective, inspiring, and knowledgeable about children and reading. This series of books is our attempt to guide teachers into a deeper understanding of their craft and art— to help already good teachers become the great teachers that we need.

Introduction

Fluency

*T*hink back to your own early literacy school experiences. How did you learn to read? What kinds of instructional activities do you recall from your elementary classrooms? Which experiences made learning to read enjoyable? Were there any that you found to be difficult or mundane? What was the role of fluency in your own instruction as a child?

Typically, teachers have difficulty recalling fluency activities that were part of their own school routines. Indeed, although a few scholars have been calling for attention to fluency since the 1980s (e.g., Allington, 1983), the 2000 report of the National Reading Panel really marked the current interest in and emphasis on fluency. In fact, we recall instructional practices from our own early education that not only didn't promote fluency, but probably discouraged it. Did you practice reading a text but only to get all the words right? Did you rush through leveled material to get to the most difficult passages as quickly as possible, for example? This "race to the finish," which was characteristic of some instructional programs, did nothing to encourage you or your peers to learn to read fluently.

Current research, however, has shown the importance of addressing the development of reading fluency as part of a total reading program. It is our hope that reading this book, completing the suggested activities, and collaborating with colleagues will clarify and enhance your knowledge of fluency instruction, the role that it plays in early literacy instruction, and how to teach and assess your students' fluency ability.

As you prepare to begin this professional development program, we invite you to consider and discuss with colleagues the following items that may help frame your interpretation and application of the material in this book. Take some time now to write notes

Book Club

about these aspects of your literacy program, particularly with regard to fluency instruction:

- Describe the conditions under which you work.

  _____
  _____
  _____

- What do your students read?

  _____
  _____
  _____

- Describe the major goals of your program.

  _____
  _____
  _____

- What are the principles that ground, or serve as a rationale for, your program?

  _____
  _____
  _____

- Describe your daily schedule or classroom routine, particularly as it relates to fluency instruction.

  _____
  _____
  _____

- Describe the materials that you currently use for fluency instruction.

  _____
  _____
  _____

- Describe how your students read when they read orally.

  _____
  _____
  _____

- How are parents involved in your literacy program?

  _____

  _____

  _____

- How do you currently assess student progress in fluency?

  _____

  _____

  _____

The chapters that follow are intended to provide an organizational framework for fluency instruction that will assist you in identifying elements that are effective and offering suggestions when modifications need to be made. Chapter 1 presents an overview of current research and professional literature. Research-based answers are provided for questions such as what fluency is, why fluency instruction is important, and how instruction can be most effective. The end of the chapter invites you to analyze, clarify, extend, discuss, and apply information learned from this chapter.

Chapter 2 focuses on research-based instructional practices. General principles for early literacy instruction in fluency are presented first. Then, you are asked to use a semantic feature analysis to evaluate your own instructional practices, considering both instructional practices that are effective and those in need of fine-tuning. The strategy suggestions that follow include ideas that can form the backbone of your fluency instruction.

Chapter 3 focuses on assessment and begins by describing broad truisms of assessment that can be applied to all aspects of literacy learning. After working with these broad assessment ideas, you are asked to examine more closely your own current assessment practices in terms of both critical elements of fluency and how you assess individual students. Vignettes and questions at the end of the chapter offer opportunities for collaboration on how to address fluency-related issues. Graphic organizers are provided for goal planning, reflection, and curriculum alignment.

Chapter 4 moves beyond classroom-based strategies and considers recommendations for families to use at home to support their children's fluency development. Parents' frequently asked questions about fluency are also addressed in this chapter.

Chapter 5 provides instructional and professional resources for teaching fluency. Throughout the book you will find ample room to make notes about various aspects of planning and implementing effective fluency instruction. We encourage you to use these spaces to record insights and ideas that are particularly pertinent to your own instruction. Doing so should provide you with the kind of concrete plan of action you'll need to offer students more consistent and effective opportunities to develop their fluency.

Evidence-Based Instruction in Reading

Fluency

Fluency: What Does Research Tell Us?

*I*n 1983, Dick Allington called fluency the neglected goal of the reading program. Today, more than 20 years later, fluency has become a very hot topic, particularly among primary-level teachers. What changed? First, an accumulation of research evidence has shown the importance of fluency in overall reading achievement (e.g., Chard, Vaughn, & Tyler, 2002; Kuhn & Stahl, 2000; National Reading Panel, 2000; Rasinski & Hoffman, 2003). Literacy scholars are now convinced that fluency is related to student reading success and that effective instruction in reading must include attention to fluency. Second, experts can now see that fluency is more than oral reading and reading speed and that fluency activities need not focus only on timed-reading drills. Indeed, the research literature has provided descriptions of effective and engaging fluency activities (e.g., Martinez, Roser, & Strecker, 1999; Rasinski, Padak, Linek, & Sturtevant, 1994). In this section, we define fluency, articulate its importance, and suggest several research-based methods for improving children's reading fluency.

What Is Fluency?

Think about the last time you heard a very fluent speaker. Most likely, the speaker didn't bungle the words, but other aspects of the speaking—not just the spoken words—helped you understand the message. The speaker probably spoke in chunks or phrases that made it easy to follow him or her. Perhaps the rate of speaking was helpful—neither too slow nor too quick. Perhaps the speaker paused dramatically or used his or her voice for emphasis. A fluent speaker helps listeners understand or comprehend the spoken message. Fluency in speaking is a multidimensional concept.

Reading fluency is also a multidimensional concept (Kuhn & Stahl, 2000). Think of fluency as a bridge that connects decoding to comprehension. This bridge consists of automatizing decoding so that readers can pay attention to constructing meaning. It also consists of interpretive and prosodic reading with appropriate expression and rate. Let's take a closer look at these elements.

Decoding is part of fluent reading. Clearly, if a reader is unable to decode the words he or she sees on a page, no reading (neither fluent nor disfluent) can happen. But mere decoding accuracy is not enough. Proficient and fluent reading requires effortless or automatic decoding. Readers need to expend as little effort as possible in the decoding aspect of reading so that their finite cognitive resources can be used for constructing meaning (LaBerge & Samuels, 1974). Consider your own reading, for example; how often do you stop to analyze a word in order to decode it? Probably rarely. Like most adult readers, you recognize the vast majority of the words you encounter instantly and automatically. As a result, you can devote your cognitive energy to the task of constructing meaning and making sense of the text.

So now the fluency "bridge" has two supports—both accurate decoding and automatic decoding. Effortless and automatic decoding, or automaticity in reading, frees the reader's cognitive capacity to work in comprehending the text—making predictions, asking questions, and creating mental images. The third support for the fluency bridge involves parsing, or chunking, the text into syntactically and semantically appropriate units and interpreting the text by reading with appropriate expression, or what linguists call *prosodic reading* (Schreiber, 1991). When a reader reads with appropriate phrasing and expression, emphasizing certain words, making extended pauses at certain points, speeding up in some sections and deliberately slowing down at others, active meaning construction and interpretation is evident. Indeed, we believe that one must comprehend the text in order to decide about where to chunk text and how to read it expressively.

Fluency is the ability to read expressively and meaningfully, as well as accurately and with appropriate speed. Successful reading requires readers to process the surface level of the text in order to comprehend. The goal of reading is comprehension, of course, but proficiently processing the surface level allows the reader to direct his or her attention to meaning. Reading fluency enables control over this surface-level text processing (Rasinski, 2003).

Why Is Fluency Important?

Part of the answer to this question should be evident in the definition just provided: Fluency is important because it builds a bridge that enables comprehension. In fact, research into repeated readings indicates that reading a particular passage several times, a common fluency instructional activity, leads not only to improvement on that text but also to improvements in decoding, reading rate, prosodic reading, and comprehension on unfamiliar texts (Dowhower, 1987, 1994; Herman, 1985; Koskinen & Blum, 1984, 1986; Kuhn & Stahl, 2000; National Reading Panel, 2000; Rasinski & Hoffman, 2003). The reading practice transfers to new, unread text. So, fluency is important because it affects comprehension.

Unfortunately, studies have also found that significant numbers of students are not fluent readers. The large-scale National Assessment of Educational Progress study (Pinnell et al., 1995), for example, concluded that 45 percent of U.S. fourth-graders read below minimally acceptable fluency levels. Only 13 percent of these fourth-graders read at the highest fluency level. From these results, then, we can assume fluency difficulties among approximately half of the primary-level population. We can also assume that nearly all primary-level students will benefit from fluency instruction.

A study of struggling elementary-level readers found similar fluency difficulties (Rasinski & Padak, 1998). In this study we conducted diagnostic assessments of all students in an urban district who had been referred by their classroom teachers for Title I support. The diagnosis focused on word decoding, fluency, and comprehension. We found students' decoding and comprehension abilities to be slightly below grade level, as might be expected by their Title I referral status. Students' fluency, however, was much more problematic. Children's oral reading was very, very slow and labored; anyone listening to these children read knew that they were struggling.

Why is fluency important? Research has shown a relationship between fluency and comprehension, the ultimate goal of reading. Moreover, studies of primary-level students' fluency have shown that significant numbers have fluency problems. These two findings point to the importance of focusing on fluency in your reading curriculum. Next, we offer some research-based ways to accomplish this.

How Can I Help Students Become Fluent Readers?

Book Club

The first steps in planning a fluency component for your reading program involve looking at your current emphasis on fluency and ensuring that reading materials are appropriate for students. These questions may help you assess your current practices:

- Are you currently devoting 15 to 20 minutes each day to fluency instruction?

  _____

  _____

  _____

  _____

- Do students have additional opportunities within each school day to practice fluent reading?

  _____

  _____

  _____

  _____

- Does your parent involvement program include sufficient attention to fluency?

  _____

  _____

  _____

  _____

- What kinds of materials do your students read? Texts read independently should be very easy for children. If students have a scaffolded opportunity to practice and rehearse, you can challenge them with material that is a bit more difficult. It's important to remember, though, that anyone's ability to read fluently depends to some extent on the difficulty of the material and the reader's familiarity with it.

  _____

  _____

  _____

  _____

To some extent, instruction in reading fluency also depends on student need. Later in this book we describe several ways to assess students' fluency. Students with decoding difficulties require instruction in that area, which is the topic of another book in this series. These students can also benefit from fluency instruction, but you will want to provide extra assistance and relatively easy materials to ensure their success. Here we describe several methods for developing students' strength in automaticity and prosodic reading (Rasinski & Padak, 2001, 2004).

Model Fluent Reading

It is essential that you model fluent reading for students. Some students are not aware that they are not fluent readers, and even more have never thought metacognitively about fluency—what a speaker does to enhance understanding. These students need to hear expressive and meaning-filled reading. They need to hear how fluent readers read and make meaning with their voices, and they need the opportunity to talk about the nature of fluent reading.

Teacher read-aloud can accomplish both of these goals. No doubt you already read aloud to your students each day. Transforming these read-aloud sessions into fluency development opportunities is easy. First, ensure that your read-alouds are as fluent as possible. This may involve some practice on your part. Second, vary the types of texts you select for read-aloud. Find poetry, drama, and expository texts to read to children; don't just read storybooks. The variety in text types will help students develop a more elaborate notion of fluent reading. They will learn how fluent poetry reading or expository reading sounds. Finally, find ways to draw students' attention to the ways you use your voice to promote fluent reading. In brief postreading conversations, ask questions such as:

- What did you notice about my voice?
- How did my voice help you pay attention or understand?
- How did I use my voice to show happiness (or excitement or anger or. . .)?

These brief conversations can help students develop and refine their abstract concepts about fluency.

You might also want to experiment by reading a short passage in several ways—fluently, in a word-by-word laborious manner, too quickly, and so on. Ask students to compare the renditions, to tell which one was most effective at communicating the author's message and why. This practice, too, helps develop self-awareness about fluency. In all, your reading aloud, especially when supplemented with brief conversations about fluency, aids students' development of a solid idea of the nature of fully fluent reading.

Provide Fluency Support and Assistance (Scaffolding) for Students

Hearing fluent reading is not the same as being a fluent reader. Thus, assisted reading, another method associated with fluency improvements (Kuhn & Stahl, 2000; National Reading Panel, 2000), should be an important component of your fluency program.

Several methods for assisted reading show promise. One is a simple routine that begins with reading a short text to students. This is followed by an invitation for students to follow along silently as you read aloud again. Group reading is next. Choral reading, antiphonal reading (dividing the class into groups), even choral reading in silly voices (like a robot, like a baby)—all these are effective and enjoyable. This routine provides good models of fluent reading and unobtrusive assistance for children who may need it.

Repeated reading, which may involve pairs of students' choice reading together or pairings of more fluent and struggling readers, provides another excellent scaffold for children (Eldredge, 1990; Eldredge & Butterfield, 1986; Eldredge & Quinn, 1988; Topping, 1987a, 1987b, 1989, 1995). Partners spend 5 or 10 minutes several times each week reading together. One child reads while the other listens. The listener offers positive comments about the reader's fluency. Then the pairs switch roles.

Your own coaching or feedback is another form of assistance. As students are practicing, alone or in pairs, stroll around the room to listen. Talk with students about what you hear:

- You got all the words right, but you read so fast! It was hard for me to follow you.
- I really like how you paused between sentences. This gave me a chance to think about the author's message.
- I loved how you used your voice in this section! You really sounded angry.
- What is this passage about? How can you tell it with your voice as well as with the words?

This sort of assistance helps students become aware of their own interpretations and moves them toward deeper levels of meaning. It also provides a good model for children's own response to partners.

Listening to books on tape while reading them silently is yet another way to provide assistance (Carbo 1978a, 1978b, 1981; Chomsky, 1976; Pluck, 1995). This is a good choice for a listening center activity. It may also provide another authentic audience for practice—students can create the taped books for others to enjoy. Assisted reading of this kind has been found to be a powerful strategy for improving fluency and comprehension.

Finally, assessment can provide a scaffold for students. Use some of the informal assessment activities described later in this book to track changes in students' accuracy, rate, and prosodic reading over time. Be sure to share this good fluency news with your students. Tangible evidence of reading improvement is a strong motivator for many students, particularly those who have not experienced much success in reading.

Encourage Repeated Readings

Practice leads to fluency in reading in the same way it does in other areas, such as driving a car or playing a musical instrument. In reading, we call this practice *repeated readings* (Samuels, 1979), which, as we noted earlier, has been found to improve reading both on the practice passages and on unfamiliar texts (Dowhower, 1987, 1994; Herman, 1985; Koskinen & Blum, 1984, 1986; Kuhn & Stahl, 2000; National Reading Panel, 2000).

Repeated readings work best when students have an authentic reason for practicing a text several times. Performance can supply this motivation. The invitation to perform gives students a natural reason for practicing. Moreover, comparing different oral renditions of the same text often provides opportunities for students to consider fluency abstractly. You can encourage this by asking students to reflect on questions such as:

- How was your second (or third or fourth) reading of this text better?
- What did you do differently with your voice? How did this change make the reading better?
- What will you do with your voice the next time to make the reading even better?

If we accept the idea of performance providing the motivation for repeated readings, then we need to consider the types of texts that lend themselves to performance. Texts meant to be read aloud with appropriate expression—such as poetry, scripts, speeches, monologues, dialogues, and jokes or riddles—are perfect for fluency development. Storybooks may be good choices for fluency practice too, especially if students will read them to a younger audience. Perhaps you can team with a kindergarten class in a "buddy reading" program.

Of course, if students are asked to practice a text for performance, they also need opportunities to perform for an audience. Many teachers we know have "fluency Fridays"; they devote some time, usually on Friday afternoons, for students to perform the texts they have been so diligently practicing throughout the week. Some teachers convert their classrooms into poetry cafes; others have Readers' Theater festivals. Parents are often invited to attend these performances. Buddy reading, whether for younger children or other school buddies (the principal, volunteers, the custodian, the librarian), may happen as well.

To benefit from repeated readings, students need consistent opportunities to practice. Persuading students to read a text repeatedly can become a dilemma unless you can provide real reasons for doing so. So, this part of your fluency program must include performance opportunities. Think of these as the equivalent of publication in the writing program. Find ways for your students to share their newly developed fluency abilities with interested and enthusiastic audiences.

Develop a Fluency Routine

All these ideas will be most effective when you bundle them into a predictable routine. Plan to devote 15 minutes (or so) to fluency everyday. Think about how best to model fluent reading, offer assisted reading opportunities, and engage students in repeated reading. Be sure to think about the assessments for this routine as well—how will you know that your efforts are paying off in increased fluency?

Several instructional routines for developing reading fluency have been developed and have shown great promise for improving reading in all readers. Fluency Oriented Reading Instruction (Stahl, Heubach, & Cramond, 1997) has students engage in modeled, repeated, and assisted reading of passages from basal readers. The Fluency Development Lesson (Rasinski & Padak, 2005; Rasinski et al., 1994) uses poetry, monologues, dialogues, speeches, and other performance texts to promote reading fluency. Fast Start (Padak & Rasinski, 2004a, 2004b, 2005; Rasinski, 1995; Stevenson, 2002) promotes early reading fluency through parental involvement. Research has shown that each of these is effective in promoting children's fluency growth and overall reading achievement.

Whether you use one of these already developed fluency routines or create your own, keep the definition of fluency presented at the beginning of this section in mind as you work with students: Fluency is the ability to read expressively and meaningfully, as well accurately and with appropriate speed. Don't concentrate solely on increasing rate of reading. In fact, emphasizing speed at the expense of prosodic and meaningful reading leads to fast readers who understand little of what they have read. So keep the focus on meaningful interpretation, and strive for ways to weave fluency work into other areas of the school curriculum.

Professional Development Suggestions

ACED: Analysis, Clarification, Extension, Discussion

I. REFLECTION (10 to 15 minutes)

ANALYSIS:

- What, for you, were the most interesting and/or important ideas in the fluency introduction and literature review presentation?

  _____

  _____

  _____

  _____

- What information was new to you?

  _____

  _____

  _____

  _____

CLARIFICATION:

- Did anything surprise you? Confuse you?

  _____

  _____

  _____

  _____

EXTENSION:

- What questions do you have?

  _____

  _____

  _____

  _____

II. DISCUSSION (20 minutes)

- Form groups of 4 to 6 members.
- Appoint a *facilitator (timer)* and *recorder*.
- Share responses. Make sure that each person has shared his or her responses to each category (Analysis/Clarification/Extension).
- Help each other with any areas of confusion.
- Answer and/or discuss questions raised by group members.
- On chart paper, the Recorder should summarize the main discussion points and identify issues or questions the group would like to raise for general discussion.

III. APPLICATION (10 minutes)

- Based on your reflection and discussion, how might you apply what you have learned from the fluency introduction and literature review?

_____

_____

_____

_____

Instructional Strategies for Fluency Development

Guiding Principles for Instruction

After years of teaching kindergarten and primary grades, Ms. Arabia expects a wide range of developmental levels and literacy foundations among young students. Some children enter school from literacy-rich home environments where they've been immersed in language and books. They can recite common children's poems, for example, and they have favorite storybooks. Others arrive in her classroom from homes where literacy has not been emphasized and their exposure to fluent reading has been limited. A growing number of kindergarten and primary-level children have native languages other than English. For all these reasons, Ms. Arabia knows that she needs differentiated instructional plans for fluency instruction. She also knows that young children are not very successful working independently, especially at the beginning of the year, so her fluency instructional routines need to reflect this reality as well.

In order to provide instruction that supports children's fluency development, then, Ms. Arabia first decided on a number of instructional routines. In deciding about the routines, she made certain that together, they would reflect important principles for fluency instruction:

- Children need to hear models of fluent reading.
- Children need support to develop fluency. This can take the form of teacher coaching, assisted reading, or both. Children also benefit from opportunities to think and talk metacognitively about fluency.
- Children need regular opportunities to practice texts. This repeated reading works best when performance is the reason for the practice.

When she taught kindergarten, Ms. Arabia's daily fluency instruction incorporated two major routines: teacher read-aloud, coupled with occasional chats with children about how she had used her voice to help children understand the text, and an assisted reading routine that featured (1) teacher reading an easy text, (2) teacher reading while children followed along using an enlarged version of the text, (3) choral reading, and (4) various types of antiphonal reading (boys vs. girls, front of the group vs. back of the group, etc.). She devoted approximately 10 to 15 minutes to fluency activity each day.

Several years ago, Ms. Arabia moved to second grade. She knew that fluency was still an important instructional emphasis, and she believed that the same three principles (modeling, support, repeated readings) could still be useful for planning her program. However, she also knew that many of her students would be reading independently and therefore might not benefit from the whole-group assisted reading routine that had worked so well in kindergarten. So her new plans involved slightly different routines: teacher read-aloud, the Fluency Development Lesson (see explanation that follows) with three different levels of text for each week, and Readers' Theater (see explanation that follows) activities. Again, she devoted approximately 15 minutes per day to fluency instruction.

We suspect that if Ms. Arabia changed grades again, she would again think about her students' needs and the three broad principles of fluency instruction to develop fluency routines. Having the principles firmly in mind facilitates the development of instruction.

Professional Development Suggestions

Evaluating Your Own Instruction

Before adding new strategies and activities to your instructional repertoire, it is important to evaluate your current teaching practices: What current instructional practices do you find to be effective? What instructional areas need to be fine-tuned? Are there instructional components that are not being covered to the degree that they need to be?

To help you in evaluating your current instructional practices, consider the accompanying semantic feature analysis chart. Along the side of the chart, you will see space for you to list those instructional strategies that you currently use to enhance children's fluency development. Across the top of the chart, you will see components that may be present in the activities that you listed. Of course, not every component can, or should, be part of every activity. Some activities will encourage students to interact with classmates, for example; others may invite a more independent response. The key is to seek a balance in terms of the variety of strategies used so that a range of developmental levels and diverse learner needs can be effectively addressed.

Take the time to complete the semantic feature analysis. Place a + sign in the corresponding box for each attribute that is present in a fluency instructional activity that you currently use. More than one attribute may be present for each activity that you list. You may wish to collaborate with colleagues, as doing so often may help you recall

16
....

CHAPTER 2

*Instructional
Strategies for
Fluency
Development*

the additional fluency strategies that you use doing the course of the school year.

When the semantic feature analysis is complete, it should help you see which aspects of fluency instruction currently receive a great deal of attention in your classroom and which aspects may not currently receive enough emphasis. Knowing this will help you to better plan adjustments in your instructional routine. Discuss your findings and insights with colleagues.

Semantic Feature Analysis for Current Fluency Instructional Practices

Fluency Strategies	Modeling	Scaffolding: Assisted Reading	Scaffolding: Coaching	Paired Reading	Repeated Reading	Performance

Strategy Suggestions

The fluency development strategies described in this section have all been found effective through research. In general, each can be adapted to work successfully with children in grades K–3 (and beyond); moreover, most can be adapted to work with different kinds of text. In the descriptions we indicate common procedures and materials, but you should feel free to innovate!

Choral/Antiphonal Reading

Purpose:

To practice reading fluently in a supportive environment; to provide a platform for exploration of prosody (speed, pitch, tone, etc.) and its effect on fluency.

Materials:

Poetry works particularly well for either activity. For antiphonal reading, you may want to seek out poems that have repetitive or accumulative patterns (e.g., a stanza or two from "I Know an Old Lady"). Some poems are written for two voices (e.g., Paul Fleischman's *Joyful Noise* or Mary Ann Hoberman's *You Read to Me; I'll Read to You*) and can easily be adapted for antiphonal reading.

Procedures:

1. Make an enlarged version of the text on chart paper or an overhead transparency. Find a yardstick or an old pointer (if chart paper) or use a pencil (if overhead) so that you can help children pace their reading.

2. Begin the session by reading the text aloud to children. You may want to ask about aspects of your reading.

3. Next, ask students to follow along silently (or in a whisper) while you read the text again. Use the pointer to help children keep pace.

4. Now have children read chorally along with you. Again, use the pointer for pacing.

5. You may want to invite children to repeat the text using different voices (read like a baby, read like a robot, whisper read, read in very loud voices, read like they're angry, etc.). You may also

want to try asking children to begin reading in a whisper, gradually increasing the volume of their voices (or the reverse).

6. If your goal is antiphonal reading (multiple readers who alternate their reading), begin with the choral reading steps 1–4. As children are becoming accustomed to antiphonal reading, you may want to assist them by color-coding the text. You could underline part 1 in red, part 2 in green, and so forth. You may also want to "conduct" the antiphonal readings for a while, again until children become accustomed to it.

7. Play with different methods of antiphonal reading: Ask children to stand or raise their hands while they read their parts, or try "snowball" reading with one child reading the first line, two the second, and so on, until the entire class is reading.

Fluency Development Lesson

Purpose:

To provide instruction and practice in a short routine that maximizes both principles of effective fluency instruction and opportunities for authentic reading.

Materials:

Use short (50 to 150 words) passages that lend themselves to oral reading. Poetry, snippets of dialogue from longer selections, parts of speeches, and so on, work well.

Procedures:

1. Distribute copies of text to each student.

2. Read the text aloud to students while they follow along silently with their own copies.

3. Discuss text content and/or prosodic qualities of reading.

4. Read the text chorally several times. (Antiphonal or echo reading is also possible.)

5. Divide the class into pairs. Each person reads the text to his or her partner three times, after which partners change roles. The listeners provide positive feedback.

6. Regroup the class. Ask for volunteers (individuals or pairs) to read the text aloud.

7. Ask students to take the text home to read aloud to family members and friends.

Paired Reading

Purpose:

To provide individual fluency support.

Materials:

Anything the student wants to read.

Procedures:

1. The student selects a book.
2. The student and a good reader (classmate, older student, volunteer, parent, etc.) read the book aloud and together.
3. The student and the good reader decide on a signal (e.g., tap) to indicate that the student wishes to read alone. If the student wishes to read alone, the good reader follows silently. If the student makes a mistake, the good reader joins in again.
4. The good reader's voice slightly leads if the student needs a great deal of support. The good reader's voice slightly follows if the student needs little support.
5. The student logs paired-reading activities (length of time, pages read, assessment of ability, etc.).

Readers' Theater

Purpose:

To provide an authentic and purposeful group oral reading experience

Materials:

Use all or part of anything written in the form of a script, including short plays available in instructional materials, plays obtainable online (see Resources in Chapter 5 and Appendix A), or trade books written in script format (e.g., Angela Johnson's *Tell Me a Story, Mama*; Donald Hall's *I Am the Dog; I Am the Cat*; Mary Ann Hoberman's *You Read to Me; I'll Read to You* series).

20
....

CHAPTER 2

*Instructional
Strategies for
Fluency
Development*

Highly able upper-primary students and older students of any ability level may transform favorite stories into scripts. Simple stories that feature lots of dialogue work best. Small groups of children can read a favorite story, decide on characters and narrator(s), and use as much of the original author's language as they wish in developing their own script. You may want to remind children that in Readers' Theater, they have only their voices to communicate meaning, so the words used in their scripts will be important. When the script is finished, make copies so each child in the group has one.

Procedures:

1. Divide the children into groups, or allow them to select their own groups. Some teachers call these "repertory groups." Group members may have varying abilities.

2. Ask each group to select a script.

3. Ask the groups to read their scripts and cast roles. Remind the children that (a) narrator roles can be divided among several children (narrator #1, narrator #2, etc.) and (b) they may use only their voices to convey meaning when they perform their scripts—no costumes, props, action, scenery, and so forth.

4. Provide the groups with ample time to practice. Some teachers do this at a set time during the day for everyone. Others encourage students to practice at free times during the school day. Remind the children to give their cast mates honest feedback.

5. Perform! Have Readers' Theater Fridays once or twice a month. (Alternatively, you may wish to have a performance each week, so you could put the groups in a rotation.) Consider taking the performances "on the road" as well—to other classrooms, for the parent-teacher organization, on the public address system, and so on.

Poetry Cafes

Purpose:

To provide authentic opportunities to practice fluency; to enhance students' understanding and enjoyment of poetry.

Materials:

Poetry anthologies with age-appropriate poetry; single poems obtained on the Web. (See Chapter 5 for books and websites.)

Procedures:

1. Display all poetry resources on Monday. Provide time for students to select the poems they wish to read during the Poetry Café (to be held on Friday afternoon). Students may also select poems of their own. Individuals, pairs, or small groups may work with a single poem.

2. Provide practice time during the week. As with Readers' Theater, this may be at a set time each day, or you may want to encourage children to use their free time to practice their poetry.

3. On the Friday afternoon of the Poetry Café, dim the lights and create a café atmosphere, to the extent possible. A music stand or lectern can be provided for students who wish to use it. Invite students to read their poems to classmates. After each poem is read and the audience applauds, invite a positive comment or two about the reader's fluency.

Tape-Recorded Reading

Purpose:

To provide individual and independent practice in fluency.

Materials:

Books with accompanying audiotapes. The tapes can be commercially produced, such as those that can be checked out from a library. An alternative is to develop a classroom listening library by having students prepare tape-recorded versions of classroom books for their peers to read.

Procedures:

1. Create a listening center in the classroom. Headphones and tape recorders will work best.

2. Stock the listening center with engaging texts/tapes for students to read while they listen.

3. Provide students with 15 to 20 minutes per day at the listening center.

4. Help students select books that are (a) written at their instructional levels and (b) very likely to be engaging for students.

5. Remind students to follow along in the text as they listen.

6. Students may want to log the pages they read during each session.

Radio Reading

Purpose:

To provide an authentic reason to practice reading; to provide an authentic reason to listen to another child read.

Materials:

A short prose selection, either fiction or nonfiction.

Procedures:

1. The child who will read to others needs to (a) practice the selection until it can be read fluently and (b) develop two or three questions about the selection to ask fellow students.
2. Small groups (three or four children each) listen to each other read. After each reading, the questions are asked and answered.

Buddy Reading

Purpose:

To provide an authentic reason to practice reading; to develop readers' self-esteem; to provide listeners with good models of oral reading.

Materials:

Texts selected by the younger of the buddy pairs.

Procedures:

1. Pair up students from two grades. Before Buddy Reading officially begins, you may want to provide pairs with opportunities to get to know each other and each others' interests.
2. The teacher of the younger class helps children select books for their buddies to read.
3. The teacher of the older class provides these books and time for older buddies to practice. Discussions about how to hold books so that younger children can see the illustrations and how to talk productively about the content of the books may be useful.

4. Once each week or two, the buddy pairs get together for reading sessions. After each session, the routine begins anew.

5. Optional: Buddies may want to become pen pals.

Timed Readings

Purpose:

To show children tangible benefits of repeated readings.

Materials:

Short text that is slightly difficult for the child to read, tape recorder and cassette tape, stopwatch, simple graph (see sample).

Words per Minute	First Reading	Second Reading	Third Reading	Fourth Reading
100				
90				
80				
70				
60				
50				
40				
30				
20				
10				

Procedures:

1. Before you begin this activity and at times throughout it, remind the children that reading fluently involves much more than reading quickly. You might want to demonstrate this either by reading something yourself much too quickly or by playing a cassette tape with the speed turned up very high.

2. Explain that "practice makes perfect." Invite discussion of other times when children have grown in skill through practice—

riding bicycles, swimming, and so on. Help them understand that the same is true of reading.

3. Ask children to work in pairs. One child reads first while the other uses the stopwatch; then they trade roles. Each child reads the text selected for him or her four times. After each reading, the partners complete the graph showing the child's speed. At the end of the four readings, the partners examine the graph to see how the fourth reading was different from the first.

4. Partners change roles and start the procedure anew.

Although becoming fluent readers is an important goal in any reading program, it's only one of several emphases in a total literacy program. Students who need additional support to develop fluency will benefit from paired reading or reading while listening. All primary-level students can benefit from routines such as the Fluency Development Lesson, Readers' Theater, and the Poetry Cafe. From 10 to 15 minutes devoted to fluency each day can yield important benefits in reading achievement.

Some combination of whole-class instruction and focused individualized work is probably the best way to conceive of the fluency portion of your reading program. Consider the diverse needs of your students when making specific plans. Evidence-based strategies and instructional guidelines, such as those discussed in this chapter, can provide you with direction for effective fluency instruction.

Fluency Materials and Programs

Materials for fluency instruction and practice are abundant. Look through children's poetry anthologies, for example. If you use a basal reading program, look for plays that can be performed as Readers' Theater. Several websites are listed in Chapter 5; these are a treasure trove of poetry, songs, jump-rope rhymes, and scripts that children will enjoy.

Commercial programs that focus on fluency are also available. In evaluating these, we recommend that you focus on the following questions:

- Is the program based on an accurate definition of fluency?
- Is the program intended for the range of readers that you teach?

- Will children find texts engaging? Are texts meant to be read aloud?
- Is the amount of time per day appropriate (10 to 15 minutes daily)?
- Is the overall instructional routine appropriate?
- Is attention paid to teacher modeling?
- Are a variety of scaffolding practices available for children who need it?
- Is performance stressed?
- Are assessment ideas offered?

Discussion Questions

Work with two other teachers, ideally ones at your own grade level. First, select two issues from the list that follows. Then, each of you should make individual notes about the issue. Third, share these notes with each other. Spend some time talking through the issue. See if you can reach consensus about how to resolve it. Make notes about this discussion. Finally, share insights with others in your whole group.

1. How can we evaluate the usefulness of our current materials for fluency instruction?

   _____

   _____

   _____

   _____

2. How can we address the tension between being "on grade level" and the repeated readings necessary to become fluent readers, especially for struggling readers?

   _____

   _____

   _____

   _____

3. What sorts of performance activities will work well for our students? What details about them need attention before we begin?

   _____

   _____

   _____

   _____

4. How can we explain our fluency program to parents?

   _____

   _____

   _____

   _____

CHAPTER 3

Assessing Fluency Development

Big Ideas

In each of the books in this series, we have identified several "big ideas" to guide your thinking about assessment. These big ideas apply to assessing all aspects of literacy learning (indeed, to all learning), but the comments and examples below frame them in the context of assessing children's fluency.

- *Focus on critical information.* Aim for a direct connection between what you need to know and the assessment tools/strategies you use. You can decide about critical information by considering the broad definition of fluency presented earlier in this book in light of your own students. It may also help to think about a student who is magnificently fluent. Try making a list of observable indicators: What would he or she do? Say? How would his or her reading sound? Having thought about the abstract definition and your own students, you can then decide on critical information. McTighe and Wiggins (2004) suggest that this process works best when it begins at the end: (1) if the desired result is for learners to____, (2) then assessment should provide you with evidence of____, (3) and so assessment tasks need to include something like____.

- *Look for patterns of behavior.* Rob Tierney (1998) notes that assessment "should be viewed as ongoing and suggestive, rather than fixed or definitive" (p. 385). No one instance can possibly tell you what you need to know about a child's fluency. Moreover, no fluent reader always reads fluently. Situations make a difference, as do practice, difficulty level of the material, and a host of other factors. (If you doubt this, imagine yourself reading something unfamiliar and difficult aloud to a large group of strangers.) So, your goal should be to determine children's fluency by finding patterns of fluent behavior. To do this, you need a plan. Get baseline information about children at the beginning of the year. Then select a few children on which to focus each week. Watch them during fluency instruction and practice. Make notes about what you observe. Some of this will be routine, but you may also want to select children about whom you need more information or children whose current behavior is surprising in some way (Rasinski & Padak, 2004).

- *Recognize developmental progressions (can't, can sometimes, can always) and attend to children's cultural or linguistic differences.* Tierney (1998) advises that "assessment should be more developmental and sustained than piecemeal and shortsighted" (p. 384). "I envision . . .

assessments that build upon, recognize, and value rather than displace what students have experienced in their worlds" (p. 381). Your plans should be sensitive to both of these issues. With regard to the former, for example, children may develop a general notion of fluency before they are able to talk about its component parts (e.g., phrasing, prosody). Likewise, they may be able to recognize fluent reading before they can produce it. With regard to the latter, cultural differences may influence some aspects of performance (e.g., eye contact), so it will be important to know about the nonverbals your students have learned at home and in their communities.

• *Be parsimonious.* The question: How much assessment information do you need? The answer: Enough to help you make good instructional decisions. One way to conceptualize this quantity-of-information question is to think in terms of three related layers of assessment information, as shown below.

At the top of the figure is what is done for and with all students in the class. Begin with a broad plan to assess children's fluency at the beginning of the year and then, perhaps, reassess quarterly. Then think about results—what (or who) do you still have questions about? This is the point to move to the second layer of the triangle. Here, you will do more focused (and time-consuming) fluency assessments. You might work individually with a child, perhaps more

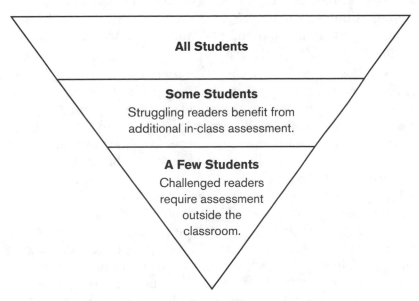

Source: Rasinski and Padak (2004, p. 277). Reprinted by permission of Pearson Education, Inc.

of what you've already done or a "deeper" assessment. For example, you might assess a child's fluency with easier material or in assisted situations (where you model fluent reading of the text and read it chorally with the child before asking him or her to read it alone). If you still have questions, don't hesitate to ask for outside help. A child or two in the class may benefit from a diagnosis by a reading specialist or other highly specialized professional. Don't delay and don't hesitate. Every lost day represents lost opportunities for that child's learning. Above all, keep assessments at these different layers related to one another, focused on the same key fluency issues.

• *Use instructional situations for assessment purposes.* Tierney (1998) notes that, ideally, "assessments should emerge from the classroom rather than be imposed upon it" (p. 375). We can think of two good reasons for this stance, one conceptual and the other practical. From a conceptual perspective, you want to know how children behave in typical instructional situations. After all, a major purpose of assessment is to provide instructional guidance. From a practical standpoint, gathering assessment information from instruction saves time for your teaching and children's learning. Children don't learn much of value during testing sessions. To evaluate your fluency instruction for possible assessment situations, you might begin by listing the instructional opportunities available to the children for reading fluently. Then develop a plan to capture observations about children's fluency during instruction. Above all, take Karen West's (1998) advice to heart: "I want instruction and evaluation to be in meaningful authentic contexts" (p. 550).

• *Include plans for (1) using assessment information to guide instruction and (2) sharing assessment information with children and parents.* The last step of your assessment planning might be to double-check ideas against their primary purposes: to help you teach more effectively and to communicate your insights with children and their parents. With regard to the former, it may be particularly important to think about how you can adjust instruction for children who appear to be struggling with fluency. Can you provide easier texts for them or build extra fluency support into their instructional days? Moreover, consider how you can share information about fluency with children and their parents. Knowing that they are making progress will keep children engaged in their learning. Assessment conversations are also good ways to help children develop more abstract concepts about fluent reading. And parents, of course, are both interested in their children's progress in school and frequently willing to assist in their children's education. Rob Tierney (1998) reminds us that it is important to keep parents informed, but more than that, involved: "Rather than keep the parent or caregiver at arm's length . . . , we need to embrace the concerns that parents have and the contributions they can make" (p. 380).

Evaluate Your Current Assessment Practices

The accompanying chart may help you take a careful look at your current assessment practices in fluency. To complete the chart, first list all the ways you currently assess students' fluency in the "Assessment Tool/ Strategy" column. Then consider the information each tool or strategy provides about each of the critical aspects by marking the chart: + = excellent source of information; – = some information; blank = no information. When the chart is complete, make plans for revision. Are some critical aspects receiving too much/not enough attention? Can some tools/strategies be eliminated or revised? What revisions will enhance your overall assessment strategies?

Critical Aspects: Fluency

Assessment Tool/Strategy	Rate	Accuracy	Expression	Volume/ Clarity	Eye Contact/ Gestures

Notes about revisions:

_____

_____

_____

_____

Ideas for Assessment

What did you conclude by analyzing your current strategies for assessing fluency? Perhaps you are satisfied that you have enough of the right kind of information about your students. If not, you may find some of the following ideas helpful for supplementing your plans.

Observation Chart

You can duplicate a chart like the one on the next page to use at times when children show their ability to read fluently. You can make brief notes on the chart or use some kind of symbol system, such as O = Outstanding, S = Satisfactory, and U = Unsatisfactory. Since assessing children in this way once every month or two may provide enough information, you can focus on different students each week and, over time, observe all your students.

Observation Chart

Aspects	Child's Name	Child's Name	Child's Name	Child's Name
Rate				
Accuracy				
Expression				
Volume/Clarity				
Eye Contact/ Gestures				

Aspects	Child's Name	Child's Name	Child's Name	Child's Name
Rate				
Accuracy				
Expression				
Volume/Clarity				
Eye Contact/ Gestures				

Oral Reading Fluency Scale

You can listen to children read and rate their performance against research-based standards. This rubric was developed as part of a federal research project to ascertain the fluency of U.S. fourth-graders (Pinnell et al., 1995). We have adapted it for your use.

Oral Reading Fluency Scale

5 Outstanding	Appropriate phrasing. Regressions or repetitions, if any, do not detract from presentation. Expressive. Appropriate rate. Few hesitations or stops.
4 Satisfactory	Mostly appropriate phrasing. Expressive interpretation inconsistent. Rate generally appropriate. Occasional hesitations or stops.
3 Unsatisfactory	Reads in short inappropriate phrases. Little expressive interpretation. Rate inappropriately slow. Extended hesitations and stops.
2 Unsatisfactory	Word-by-word reading. Very little or no expression or interpretation. Excessively slow (or fast) rate.
1 Unsatisfactory	Excessive word recognition errors significantly disrupt fluency and meaning.

Source: Adapted from Pinnell et al. (1995).

Oral Reading Rate Norms

Although fluency is more than reading quickly, comparing children's rates of reading against established norms can provide helpful information. To do this, simply ask the child to read for one minute. Make note of how many words the child reads correctly and compare the total to the chart on the next page. Children whose rates fall near these norms should be considered as making satisfactory progress in fluency. Children whose rates are substantially below the norms have fluency problems. Children whose rates are substantially above the norms deserve further consideration. If the reading is so rapid that the listener's understanding is impeded, a very rapid rate may be indicative of fluency problems.

Oral Reading Rate Norms

Grade	Fall	Winter	Spring
1	0–20	20–40	40–60
2	40–60	50–80	70–100
3	60–90	70–100	90–120
4	90–110	100–120	110–130
5	95–115	110–130	120–140
6	105–125	120–140	135–155

Source: Adapted from Hasbrouck and Tindal (1992) and Howe and Shin (2001).

Self-Assessment

Students can and should have some say in evaluating their own growth in fluency. In addition to fostering students' sense of responsibility for their own learning, self-assessment invites students to think metacognitively. In other words, each time they assess themselves, students think about fluency as an abstract concept. Over time, then, fluency will become part of what they naturally think about when they read. Ideas for self-assessment include:

- *Occasional conversations.* You might begin by asking students to assess your fluency after a read-aloud session: "How fluent was my reading?" "What did I do with my voice to make it easier for you to understand?" "How could I use my voice better the next time?"

- *Peer feedback.* When children are listening to each other read, encourage them to say something about their peers' reading.

- *Checklists.* You might create simple checklists for students to complete, perhaps using smiley faces as response options. Items on the list could include statements such as "I read most of the words right," "I read with good expression," "My reading sounded smooth and easy," "I spoke loud enough for people to hear me," "My voice was clear," and "My listener could understand me" (Rasinski & Padak, 2005).

- *Journal entries.* On occasion, ask children to write about their own fluency in their journals. Prompts could include some of the checklist items mentioned above.

Plans for Change

In this chapter, you have evaluated your own assessment strategies for fluency and, as a result, perhaps generated some ideas for change. Use the chart on the next page to make notes about the changes you wish to make. As you do so, make sure that these changes reflect the "big ideas" outlined at the beginning of the chapter:

- Focus on critical information.
- Look for patterns of behavior.
- Recognize developmental progressions and attend to children's cultural or linguistic differences.
- Be parsimonious. (Which of your strategies will work for all of your students? Which might be reserved for more careful attention to some students' fluency?)
- Use instructional situations for assessment purposes.
- Include plans for (1) using assessment information to guide instruction and (2) sharing assessment information with children and parents.

You may want to share your plans with others to get their feedback.

Book Club

Goal Planning: Fluency Assessment

Goal _____

Plans by _____ Date _____

Action Steps: What do I need to do?	Materials/Resources	Evaluation: How will I assess the usefulness of this change?

CHAPTER 4

Beyond Strategies

*I*n earlier chapters, we explored how children learn to become fluent readers and discussed some of the best instructional strategies to support that process. In this chapter, we will consider issues that go "beyond strategies." In particular, we address English language learners (ELLs) and provide guidelines and suggestions for at-home fluency activities.

ELL Students and Fluency Development

Did you study a foreign language in school? If so, you may recall feeling both excited and confused as you explored a whole new way of talking and thinking. This is how many children from other cultures feel as they enter U.S. classrooms. Given the cultural and linguistic diversity of the nation's population, your classroom may have children from several countries. How do you plan instruction that reaches each individual learner?

It is important to keep in mind that children raised in bilingual homes have unique advantages as well as unique challenges. These children bring rich background experiences that can be tapped to enhance everyone's learning. They know how to move between two languages, integrating sounds and meanings into new words and grammatical structures. Their natural manipulation of two languages promotes higher-level thinking. Yet, ELL students sometimes feel lost in the unfamiliar linguistic and academic world in which they find themselves. Fitzgerald and Graves (2004) describe this feeling:

> Many English-language learners bring an array of emotions to our classrooms that often are not evident on the surface. The student who is afraid that his talk will sound funny to others may hide his self-consciousness. The student who does not fully understand what is said may hold a steady gaze and outwardly appear confident or even cocky. (p. 3)

Fortunately, everything you have learned so far about how to teach fluency applies to both first and second language learners: ELL students need models of fluent reading in English as well as supported opportunities to practice activities that will enhance their fluency. The major difference is that ELL students may require more scaffolding and practice. Following are three key ideas to keep in mind as you plan instruction for second language learners.

- *Build conceptual connections through prior knowledge.* Teachers know that activating and applying prior knowledge is central to all learning: As students compare new information with what they already know, they deepen their understanding of the topic. Second language learners, however, may lack basic content or conceptual knowledge in the texts teachers ask them to read. They also may not understand the vocabulary or idioms of English. You can use discussion to relate unfamiliar topics or concepts to similar topics or concepts in ELL students' lives. You may need to preteach some vocabulary that is central to understanding the text.

- *Provide explicit models of good language use.* As you model fluent reading through read-aloud, you can introduce a wide range of genres with different textual structures. Find good, interesting literature that will expand students' textual, content, and conceptual knowledge. This is important for all learners, but it is particularly helpful to ELL students. Some cultures, for example, do not use the problem–solution story structure that is popular in many school texts. Second language learners from such cultures would not automatically draw on this familiar structural framework to support their understanding of the text's meaning. Furthermore, text selection can include topics and concepts that will give ELL students valuable background knowledge for school success. For second language learners, frequent opportunities to hear English texts read orally will build vocabulary, deepen comprehension, and model fluency.

- *Provide necessary scaffolding and support.* English language learners may benefit from additional practice or individual practice, such as listening to tape-recorded texts or paired reading. If your ELL students are working with a special teacher or tutor to learn English, make sure that he or she knows about your fluency activities and has access to the texts you use in your classroom. The English language teacher or tutor may be willing to provide more practice or to use these texts for language-learning activities.

Fluency Activities at Home

Both practitioners and researchers have long recognized the importance of parental involvement in children's early reading achievement. Children whose families encourage at-home literacy activities have higher phonemic awareness and decoding skills (Burgess, 1999), higher reading achievement in the elementary grades (Cooter, Marrin, & Mills-House, 1999), and advanced oral language development (Senechal, LeFevre, & Thomas, 1998). Family literacy professionals often point out that parents are their children's first and most important teachers. Instructing parents to simply "Read to your child" may be a start, but it is not enough. Parents need specific suggestions and guidelines about what to do and how to respond to their child's literacy development. In this section we offer guidelines and some sample activities for home involvement programs and practices that foster children's fluency development.

Teachers know that home involvement can provide rich opportunities for children to develop as readers. Moreover, it's important for children to see reading and literacy activities as worthwhile and critical outside of school as well as within school walls. Yet, home involvement programs are sometimes frustrating for teachers, parents, and children alike. Our work with supporting home involvement programs has led us to several design characteristics. These must be present for home involvement programs for young readers to be successful (Rasinski & Padak, 2004):

- *Use proven and effective strategies.* Many parents have limited time to devote to working with their children, so at-home activities must be focused on ideas that have been proven to make a positive difference in children's reading achievement.

- *Use authentic reading texts.* Reading aloud to children allows parents to model fluent reading as well as point out text features. Similarly, when parents read with their children or listen to their children read, children grow as readers. These simple activities—read to, read with, and listen to children—are powerful ways to promote reading achievement. What about texts? We believe it's essential for them to be authentic. For young readers, texts such as simple poems, song lyrics, jokes, and jump-rope rhymes work very well.

- *Provide materials.* Some parent involvement plans fail because parents lack appropriate texts or the time or resources to acquire them. The easiest solution is to provide parents and children with reading materials. In addition to looking for materials in books, teachers will find the Internet a treasure trove of wonderful materials for children and parents to read. (See resources listed in Chapter 5 for examples.)

With these principles in mind, you can develop some simple home fluency activities. Suggestions include the following:

- Talk to parents about the importance of modeling fluent reading and of talking with children about how fluent reading sounds. You might suggest that parents occasionally add these brief discussions to their read-aloud sessions.

- Show parents how to do paired reading with their children.

- Ask children to read poems or other texts to people (or pets or stuffed animals) at home. If you copy a brief text on one side of a sheet of paper, those who listen to the child read can sign their names on the other side, thus becoming members of the "Lucky Listener Club."

- Provide special support for ELL families. Classroom volunteers can record texts in English for children to take home. Together, the parent and child can listen to the recording (several times, if necessary) and then read aloud along with the taped version.

Fast Start, a more comprehensive home involvement routine we developed and have been studying for several years (Padak & Rasinski, 2004a, 2004b, 2005; Stevenson, Rasinski, & Padak, 2006) is also a highly effective way to support children's fluency development and overall reading achievement at home. The Fast Start routine has four basic steps:

1. The parent (or more able reader: sibling, grandparent, babysitter, etc.) and the child sit together. The parent reads a short text to the child several times, pointing to words as they are read.

2. The parent and the child read the text together and aloud. They do this several times.

3. The child reads the text independently. The parent listens, provides support if necessary, and praises the child's reading.

4. The parent and the child do a brief, developmentally appropriate literacy-related activity based on the text.

Texts for the Fast Start routine are short poems, jump-rope rhymes, or songs. Many resources for locating these are in Chapter 5. Activities are simple to develop. We recommend that you develop three sets of activities that can be used with any text. One set can focus

on concepts about print, a second set can address phonemic awareness issues, and the third set can relate to beginning reading. Then you
can simply tell each family which set of activities will benefit the
child most. Here are a few examples of activities.

Concepts about Print

- Ask your child to count the lines (or words) in a poem. Ask him
  or her to point at each line (or word) as it is counted.
- Ask questions about the words: "How many words are in line
  1?" "Show me the third word in line 2." "Which line has the
  most words?" "Which line has the fewest words?"
- Say a letter of the alphabet. Ask your child to find all the times
  that a particular letter is used in the poem. Repeat for several
  other letters.

Phonemic Awareness

- Say two words from the text. Ask your child to tell you if the
  words rhyme with one another. Repeat with several other pairs
  of words.
- Find a word from the text that is a simple rhyming word. Ask
  your child to say some words that rhyme with the word you
  chose. Write all these words in a list.
- Say a word from the text. Ask your child to say the word by
  breaking it into sounds. (For example, you might say *bat*, and
  your child would say /b/—/a/—/t/.) You can also do the oppo-
  site (you say /b/—/a/—/t/ and ask your child to tell you what
  word it is: *bat*).
- Say two words from the text. Ask your child if the words start
  with the same sound. Repeat several times. (Choose some words
  that do start with the same sounds and some that don't.)

Beginning Reading

- Make little cards of common words in the texts. After you have
  gathered 10 to 12 words over several days, play with them. If you
  make a duplicate set of cards, you can play "Concentration" or
  "Go Fish."
- Find words from a text that all have the same vowel. Put the
  words on word cards. Ask your child to sort the cards into cate-

gories according to the sounds that the vowel makes in the words.

- Ask your child to sort the word cards into categories according to the consonant sound that is found in the word. For example, sort your words into all the words that begin with the /b/ sound, or sort your words into all the words that end with the /k/ sound.

- Select a word from the text. Play a guessing game with it. For example, with the word *hat,* you could ask, "What word would we have if we changed the /h/ to a /p/?" "What word would we have if we put an /e/ on the end?"

Participating in Fast Start at home leads to reading achievement. Moreover, both children and parents enjoy the Fast Start routine and find it valuable (Padak & Rasinski, 2004a, 2004b; Stevenson, Rasinski, & Padak, 2006). Although its benefits extend beyond fluency, Fast Start is an excellent way to promote children's fluency development at home.

Reflection Protocol

ACED: Analysis, Clarification, Extension, Discussion

I. REFLECTION (10 to 15 minutes)

ANALYSIS:

- What, for you, were the most interesting and/or important ideas in this chapter?

  _____

  _____

  _____

  _____

- What information was new to you?

  _____

  _____

  _____

  _____

CLARIFICATION:

- Did anything surprise you? Confuse you?

  _____

  _____

  _____

  _____

EXTENSION:

- What questions do you have?

  _____

  _____

  _____

  _____

II. DISCUSSION (30 minutes)

- Form groups of 4 to 6 members.
- Appoint a *facilitator (timer)* and *recorder.*
- Share responses. Make sure that each person has shared his or her responses to each category (Analysis/Clarification/Extension).
- Help each other with any areas of confusion.
- Answer and/or discuss questions raised by group members.
- On chart paper, the Recorder should summarize the main discussion points and identify issues or questions the group would like to raise for general discussion.

III. APPLICATION (10 minutes)

- Based on your reflection and discussion, how might you apply what you have learned from this chapter?

_____

_____

_____

_____

Discussion Questions

1. Look through the poetry anthologies you have available (don't forget the Internet) to locate poems that you believe your students will enjoy. If you have English language learners, find poems especially for them. Make notes about choral or antiphonal reading activities to use with the poems.

   _____

   _____

   _____

2. Work with a colleague who also teaches at your grade level. Discuss these issues and make notes about your answers. How much fluency instruction should be whole-group oriented? How much should be small-group oriented? What kinds of groups should be formed? How much individual work should be assigned? And for all of these questions, why? After your discussion, share your ideas with others in your professional development group.

   _____

   _____

   _____

3. Work with a partner to examine the Fast Start suggestions in light of your school. Make implementation plans, including adaptations, if necessary.

   _____

   _____

   _____

4. In the *Principals' FAQ Project* (Mraz et al., 2001), principals provided questions about fluency that parents frequently asked. The questions are listed here. Work in a small group comprised of both veteran and novice teachers. Use what you have learned through this professional development program to compile responses to each question.

- Is it okay for my child to keep reading the same book again and again?

  _____

  _____

  _____

- When should I stop reading aloud to my child?

  _____

  _____

  _____

- How is oral reading assessed?

  _____

  _____

  _____

- How do children develop fluency?

  _____

  _____

  _____

  _____

5. Work with a small group (two or three other teachers). Read the following vignette and discuss the questions. Then share your ideas and insights with others in your professional development group.

Book Club

VIGNETTE

Several years ago, the Board of Education for your school district asked that the kindergarten curriculum be reviewed and, if warranted, changed. A special task force was created for this purpose. As a language arts consultant, you are part of this group. This group spent a year reviewing available research, formulating a philosophy, and establishing goals. Year 2 involved finding and, where necessary, writing curriculum and providing professional development for teachers. The new language arts curriculum is implemented in year 3. Implementation appears to proceed smoothly. Additional professional development is provided for teachers, who believe the new curriculum is effective.

In April, you receive a phone call from an elementary principal who reports a problem with some of her kindergarten parents. Several parents had met with her to "express their outrage with this new program." After investigation, the principal believes that the parents' concerns may be related to comments made by a first-grade teacher during a parent–teacher conference: "I don't know what I'll do with these children next year. All they do in kindergarten is play. They memorize little poems and say them. They don't spend much time at all with skill sheets."

QUESTIONS

- How can you help the principal with her problem?

  _____

  _____

  _____

- How should parents be kept apprised of curriculum changes? Other teachers?

  _____

  _____

  _____

- What do parents need to know about fluency? How can this information be communicated?

  _____

  _____

  _____

6. Complete one or both of the following charts with your insights and plans for fluency instruction.

Curriculum Alignment

Component	What Is. . .	What Should Be. . .
Curriculum		
Instruction		
Materials		
Assessment		
Home Connection		

Source: Adapted from Taylor and Collins (2003).

Goal Planning

Goal _____

Plans by _____ Date _____

Action Steps	Materials/Resources	Evaluation

CHAPTER 5

Resources

*I*n this final chapter, we offer resources for classroom activities and for your own further learning. Both print and Web-based resources are provided.

Websites

Florida Center for Reading Research (search on fluency; resources and reviews of commercially available materials): www.fcrr.org

Children's Poetry Online

The Children's Literature Web Guide (University of Calgary; follow links for online songs and poetry for children):
    http://ucalgary.ca/~dkbrown/storsong.html
Kidzpage: www.veeceet.com
Poetry4kids: http://poetry4kids.com
Internet School Library Media Center (poetry for children):
    http://falcon.jmu.edu/~ramseyil/poe and www.poetry-online.org/childrens_poetry_resource_index.htm
Jump-Rope Rhymes: www.gameskidsplay.net/jump_rope_rhymes/

Readers' Theater Scripts

www.storiestogrowby.com/script.html
www.aaronshep.com/rt/
http://storycart.com
http://loiswalker.com/catalog/guidesamples.html
www.teachingheart.net/readerstheater.htm
www.richmond.k12.va.us/readamillion/readerstheater.htm
www.readinglady.com/Readers_Theater/Scripts/scripts.html
www.readerstheatre.ecsd.net/collection.htm
www.timelessteacherstuff.com/
www.proteacher.com/070173.shtml
http://gvc03c32.virtualclassroom.org/ (scripts based on science experiments)
www.literacyconnections.com/ReadersTheater.html (great links to other sites)

Children's Books Written in Script Format

Fleischman, P. (2004). *Joyful Noise*. New York: Harper Trophy.

Hall, D. (1994). *I Am the Dog, I Am the Cat*. New York: Dial.

Hoberman, M. (2001). *You Read To Me, I'll Read To You: Very Short Stories to Read Together*. Boston: Little, Brown.

Hoberman, M. (2004). *You Read To Me, I'll Read To You: Very Short Fairy Tales to Read Together*. Boston: Little, Brown.

Hoberman, M. (2005). *You Read To Me, I'll Read To You: Mother Goose Tales to Read Together*. Boston: Little, Brown.

Hoose, P., & Hoose, H. (1998). *Hey, Little Ant*. Berkeley, CA: Tricycle Press.

Johnson, A. (1989). *Tell Me a Story, Mama*. New York: Orchard.

Raschka, C. (1993). *Yo? Yes!* New York: Orchard.

Poetry Books for Children

Adoff, A. (1995). *Slowdance Heartbreak Blues*. New York: Macmillan.

Cole, J., & Calmenson, S. (1995). *Yours Till Banana Splits: 201 Autograph Rhymes*. New York: Beech Tree.

dePaola, T. (1985). *Tomie dePaola's Mother Goose*. New York: Putnam.

dePaola, T. (1988). *Tomie dePaola's Book of Poems*. New York: Putnam.

deRegniers, B., Moore, E., & White, M. (1969). *Poems Children Will Sit Still For*. New York: Citation.

deRegniers, B., Moore, E., & White, M. (1988). *Sing a Song of Popcorn: Every Child's Book of Poems*. New York: Scholastic.

Hale, G. (1997). *Read-Aloud Poems for Young People*. New York: Black Dog & Leventhal.

Hopkins, L. B. (1995). *Small Talk: A Book of Short Poems*. New York: Harcourt Brace.

Lansky, B. (1994). *A Bad Case of the Giggles*. New York: Meadowbrook Press.

Lansky, B. (1996). *Poetry Party*. New York: Meadowbrook Press.

Lobel, A. (1986). *The Random House Book of Mother Goose*. New York: Random House.

Moss, J. (1989). *The Butterfly Jar*. New York: Bantam.

Moss, J. (1991). *The Other Side of the Door*. New York: Bantam.

Opie, I. (Ed.). (1996). *My Very First Mother Goose*. Cambridge. MA: Candlewick.

Patten, B. (1999). *The Puffin Twentieth Century Collection of Verse.* London: Penguin.

Prelutsky, J. (Ed.). (1983). *The Random House Book of Poetry for Children.* New York: Random House.

Prelutsky, J. (1984). *New Kid on the Block.* New York: Greenwillow.

Prelutsky, J. (Ed.). (1986). *Read-Aloud Rhymes for the Very Young.* New York: Knopf.

Prelutsky, J. (1990). *Something Big Has Been Here.* New York: Greenwillow.

Prelutsky, J. (1999). *The Twentieth Century Children's Poetry Treasury.* New York: Knopf.

Silverstein, S. (1974). *Where the Sidewalk Ends.* New York: HarperCollins.

Silverstein, S. (1981). *A Light in the Attic.* New York: HarperCollins.

Slier, D. (Ed.). (1991). *Make a Joyful Noise: Poems for Children by African-American Poets.* New York: Checkerboard.

Sword, E. (1995). *A Child's Anthology of Poetry.* Hopewell, NJ: Ecco.

Wildsmith, B. (1964). *Brian Wildsmith's Mother Goose.* New York: Franklin Watts.

Books about Readers' Theater

Barchers, Suzanne. (2000). *From Atalanta to Zeus : Readers Theatre from Greek Mythology.* Greenwood Village, CO: Teacher Ideas Press.

Barchers, Suzanne. (1993). *Reader's Theatre for Beginning Readers.* Greenwood Village, CO: Teachers Idea Press.

Barnes, James W. (2004). *Sea Songs: Readers Theatre from the South Pacific.* Greenwood Village, CO: Teacher Ideas Press.

Bauer, Caroline Feller. (1991). *Presenting Reader's Theatre.* New York: HH Wilson.

Blau, Lisa. (2000). *The Best of Reader's Theater* (volumes I and II). One From the Heart. Available online at www.lisablau.com

Braun, Win. (2000). *A Reader's Theatre Treasury of Stories.* Calgary, Aberta, Canada: Braun & Braun.

Fredericks, Anthony D. (1993). *Frantic Frogs and Other Frankly Fractured Folktales for Readers Theatre.* Greenwood Village, CO: Teacher Ideas Press.

Fredericks, Anthony D. (2001). *Readers Theatre for American History.* Greenwood Village, CO: Teacher Ideas Press.

Fredericks, Anthony D. (2002). *Science Fiction Readers Theatre.* Greenwood Village, CO: Teacher Ideas Press.

Fredericks, Anthony D. (2000). *Silly Salamanders and Other Slightly Stupid Stuff for Readers Theatre.* Greenwood Village, CO: Teacher Ideas Press.

Fredericks, Anthony D. (1997). *Tadpole Tales and Other Totally Terrific Treats for Readers Theatre.* Greenwood Village, CO: Teachers Ideas Press.

McBride-Smith, Barbara. (2001). *Tell It Together: Foolproof Scripts for Story Theatre.* Little Rock, AR: August House Publishers.

Ratliff, Gerald Lee. (1999). *Introduction to Readers Theatre: A Guide to Classroom Performance.* Colorado Springs, CO: Meriwether.

Shepard, Aaron. (2004). *Readers on Stage: Resources for Reader's Theater.* Los Angeles, CA: Shepard Publications.

Sierra, Judy. (1996). *Multicultural Folktales for the Feltboard and Readers' Theater.* Phoenix, AZ: Oryx Press.

Sloyer, Shirlee. (2003). *From the Page to the Stage: The Educator's Complete Guide to Readers' Theatre.* Greenwood Village, CO: Teacher Ideas Press/Libraries Unlimited.

Teacher Resource Books and Articles

Eldredge, J. L., & Butterfield, D. D. (1986). Alternatives to traditional reading instruction. *The Reading Teacher, 40,* 32–37.

Invernizzi, M., Juel, C., & Rosemary, C. (1996). A community volunteer tutorial that works. *The Reading Teacher, 50,* 304–311.

Koskinen, P. S., & Blum, I. H. (1986). Paired repeated reading: A classroom strategy for developing fluent reading. *The Reading Teacher, 40,* 70–75.

Koskinen, P. S., Blum, I. H., Bisson, S. A., Phillips, S. M., Creamer, T. S., & Baker, T. K. (1999). Shared reading, books, and audiotapes: Supporting diverse students in school and at home. *The Reading Teacher, 52,* 430–444.

Kuhn, M. (2004). Helping students become accurate, expressive readers: Fluency instruction for small groups. *The Reading Teacher, 58,* 333–344.

Kuhn, M. R., & Stahl, S. A. (2000). *Fluency: A Review of Developmental and Remedial Practices* (CIERA Rep. No. 2-008). Ann Arbor, MI: Center for the Improvement of Early Reading Achievement.

Martinez, M., & Roser, N. (1985). Read it again: The value of repeated readings during storytime. *The Reading Teacher, 38,* 782–786.

Martinez, M., Roser, N., & Strecker, S. (1999). "I never thought I could be a star": A Readers Theatre ticket to reading fluency. *The Reading Teacher, 52,* 326–334.

Opitz, M. F., & Rasinski, T. V. (1998). *Good-Bye Round Robin: 25 Effective Oral Reading Strategies.* Portsmouth, NH: Heinemann.

Perfect, K. A. (1999). Rhyme and reason: Poetry for the heart and head. *The Reading Teacher, 52,* 728–737.

Prescott, J. O. (2003). The power of reader's theater. *Instructor, 112*(5), 22–26+.

Rasinski, T. V. (1989). Fluency for everyone: Incorporating fluency in the classroom. *The Reading Teacher, 42,* 690–693.

Rasinski, T. V. (2000). Speed does matter in reading. *The Reading Teacher, 54,* 146–151.

Rasinski, T. V. (2003). *The Fluent Reader: Oral Reading Strategies for Building Word Recognition, Fluency, and Comprehension.* New York: Scholastic.

Rasinski, T. V., & Hoffman, T. V. (2003). Theory and research into practice: Oral reading in the school literacy curriculum. *Reading Research Quarterly, 38,* 510–522.

Rasinski, T. V., & Padak, N. (2001). *From Phonics to Fluency: Effective Teaching of Decoding and Reading Fluency in the Elementary School.* New York: Addison-Wesley, Longman.

Rasinski, T. V., & Padak, N. (2004). *Effective Reading Strategies: Teaching Children Who Find Reading Difficult* (3rd ed.). Columbus, OH: Merrill/Prentice-Hall.

Topping, K. (1987). Paired reading: A powerful technique for parent use. *The Reading Teacher, 40,* 604–614.

Topping, K. (1989). Peer tutoring and paired reading. Combining two powerful techniques. *The Reading Teacher, 42,* 488–494.

Worthy, J., & Broaddus, K. (2002). Fluency beyond the primary grades: From group performance to silent, independent reading. *The Reading Teacher, 55,* 334–343.

Worthy, J., & Prater, K. (2002). "I thought about it all night": Readers Theater for reading fluency and motivation. *The Reading Teacher, 56,* 294–297.

More Fluency Resources

Websites for Knock Knock Jokes

Pairs of students can prepare these short jokes for performance. We recommend that you examine the jokes carefully for content, concepts, and the like, before using them. Enjoy!

www.knock-knock-joke.com/knock_knock_093.htm
www.lofthouse.com/humor/knockknock/index.html
http://en.wikipedia.org/wiki/Knock-knock_joke
www.paralumun.com/jokesknockknock.htm
www.indianchild.com/knock_knock_jokes1.htm

Moving from Poem to Poetry Practice to Readers' Theater

Start with a short poem. Then think about how children could read it antiphonally. Finally, make a Readers' Theater script by including a narrator and a main character or two. Here's an example:

Jack and Jill went up the hill
To fetch a pail of water.
Jack fell down and broke his crown
And Jill came tumbling after.

Antiphonal Reading

Boys:	Jack
Girls:	and Jill
All:	went up the hill to fetch a pail of water.
Boys:	Jack fell down and broke his crown
Girls:	and Jill came tumbling after.
All:	OUCH!!

Readers' Theater

Characters:	Narrator, Jack, Jill
Narrator:	Once upon a time, there were a brother and a sister.
Jack:	I'm Jack.
Jill:	I'm Jill.
Narrator:	Their dad asked them to fetch a pail of water.
Jack:	What does "fetch" mean?
Jill:	I think it means "get."
Jack:	OK, let's go up the hill. We can find water there.
Narrator:	So Jack and Jill went up the hill to fetch a pail of water.
Jill:	This looks slippery. Watch out, Jack!
Narrator:	Poor Jack fell down.
Jack:	And I broke my crown!
Jill:	That means his head, but he only bumped it.
Narrator:	And Jill came tumbling after.
Jack:	We both rolled down the hill.
Jill:	And we spilled the water!

Books to Make into Scripts

These simple books will be easy to recast into scripts. Each also features the predictable patterns that will support children's beginning attempts as readers.

Brown, M. (1947). *Goodnight moon.* New York: Harcourt.
Carle, E. (1969). *The very hungry caterpillar.* New York: Philomel.
Eastman, P. D. (1960). *Are you my mother?* New York: Random House.
Fox, M. (1987). *Hattie and the fox.* New York: Bradbury.
Gag, W. (1928). *Millions of cats.* New York: Coward-McCann.
Hutchins, P. (1986). *The doorbell rang.* New York: Greenwillow.
Keats, E. J. (1971). *Over in the meadow.* New York: Scholastic.
Marshall, E. (1994). *Fox in love.* New York: Puffin.
Martin, B. (1983). *Brown bear, brown bear.* New York: Holt.
Minarik, E. (1957). *Little bear.* New York: Harper and Row.
Rosen, M. (1992). *We're going on a bear hunt.* New York: Atheneum.
Sendak, M. (1963). *Where the wild things are.* New York: Scholastic.

Websites for Song Lyrics

A routine for using lyrics might begin with children singing the song with you. Then you can show them an enlarged version of the printed lyrics and ask them to read along with you without singing. Songs that have hand motions (see www.preschooleducation.com for many great examples) are perfect for Readers' Theater.

www.kididdles.com/lyrics/allsongs.html
www.bussongs.com/
www.mamalisa.com/world/ (songs and nursery rhymes from around the
    world)
http://falcon.jmu.edu/~ramseyil/songs.htm
www.preschooleducation.com/song.shtml

Readers' Theater Scripts

Mary Had a Little Lamb

Mary had a little lamb.
Its fleece was white as snow.
And everywhere that Mary went,
The lamb was sure to go.

It followed her to school one day,
Which was against the rule.
It made the children laugh and play
To see a lamb at school.

Parts (7): Narrator, Mary, lamb, teacher,
children at school (3)

Narrator: Mary had a little lamb.

Mary: That's right. I do. She is my pet. She's very pretty.

Lamb: Bah bah bah. Thank you.

Narrator: Its fleece was white as snow.

Lamb: Bah bah bah. My fleece is my fur. It is very white.

Mary: I think her fleece looks like cotton or clouds.
Snow, too.

Narrator: And everywhere that Mary went,
The lamb was sure to go.

Mary: That's right. She follows me everywhere!

Lamb: Bah bah bah. I like to go with Mary. It is fun to
follow her around.

Narrator: You're not going to believe this—It followed her
to *school* one day.

Mary: She did. Can you believe it? She walked right in
the school with me. Then she walked into my
classroom!

Narrator: Which was against the rule.

Teacher: That's right. No animals in school. That is one of our rules.

Mary: I told the teacher I was sorry. But what can I do? My lamb follows me everywhere.

Narrator: It made the children laugh and play
To see a lamb at school.

Children: Wow! Look at that! Mary's lamb walked right into our classroom. That's funny! A lamb at school!

Lamb: Bah bah bah. Will someone read me a story, please?

All: The End.

Two Birds

Parts (4): Narrator, bird #1, bird #2, stone

Narrator: There were two birds sat on a stone.

All: fa, la, la, la, lal, de

Bird #1: One flew away, and then there was one.

All: fa, la, la, la, lal, de

Bird #2: The other bird flew after
And then there was none.

All: fa, la, la, la, lal, de

Stone: And so the stone
Was left alone.

All: fa, la, la, la, lal, de

Simple Simon

Simple Simon met a pieman
Going to the fair.
Says Simple Simon to the pieman,
"Let me taste your ware."

Says the pieman to Simple Simon,
"Show me first your penny."
Says Simple Simon to the pieman,
"Indeed, I have not any."

Parts (3): Narrator, Simple Simon, pieman

Narrator:	Once upon a time, Simple Simon went for a walk.
Simple Simon:	It is such a nice day. I think I will walk to the fair.
Narrator:	Simple Simon walked for a long time.
Simple Simon:	Gosh! I have been walking a long time. I am getting a little hungry.
Narrator:	Simple Simon met a pieman.
Simple Simon:	Wow! What is that good smell? I am really hungry!!
Pieman:	Hello. I sell pies.
Simple Simon:	Let me taste your pies, please.
Pieman:	OK, but you can't taste them for free. First show me your money.
Simple Simon:	Alas, I don't have any money.
Pieman:	Sorry, then. You can't have any pie.
Simple Simon:	Oh rats! I am so hungry.
Pieman:	OK, maybe just a little taste.

Simple Simon: Apple pie, please. And do you have any ice cream?

All: The End.

Humpty Dumpty

Humpty Dumpty sat on a wall.
Humpty Dumpty had a great fall.
All the king's horses and all the king's men
Couldn't put Humpty together again.

Parts (2, but 4 children): Humpty Dumpty, king's men
(3 children in unison)

Humpty Dumpty: Here I am sitting on a wall. It is a nice day. The sun is out. The birds are singing.

King's Men: Gallop, gallop, gallop.

Humpty Dumpty: I am so happy. I think I will swing my legs. KA—BOOM!!

King's Men: Did you hear that loud noise?

Humpty Dumpty: Oh no! I fell. Ouch! OW!! Ouch! OW!!

King's Men: We should find out about the noise. Let's go! Gallop, gallop, gallop.

Humpty Dumpty: Ouch! OW!! Ouch! OW!!

King's Men: Look! It is Humpty Dumpty. He must have fallen off the wall.

Humpty Dumpty: Ouch! OW!! Ouch! OW!!

King's Men: Let's put him back together again.

Humpty Dumpty: Ouch! OW!! Ouch! OW!!

King's Men: We can't put him back together again. We should take him to the doctor. Let's go!

Humpty Dumpy: Ouch! OW!! Ouch! OW!! Thank you!

All: The End.

Old Mother Hubbard

Old Mother Hubbard
Went to the cupboard
To get her poor dog a bone.
But when she got there,
The cupboard was bare.
And so the poor dog had none.

Parts (3): Narrator, Old Mother Hubbard, Dog

Narrator:	Old Mother Hubbard Went to the cupboard To get her poor dog a bone.
Old Mother Hubbard:	My dog is so good. She slept on my lap. She let me pet her. I will get her a bone.
Dog:	Oh, Yummy! I love bones.
Narrator:	But when she got there, The cupboard was bare.
Old Mother Hubbard:	Goodness! Where are the bones? I don't see anything in here. No bones for the dog. No food for me!
Narrator:	And so the poor dog had none.
Dog:	Oh, no! And I was very hungry.
Old Mother Hubbard:	I guess I should go to the grocery store.
Dog:	Oh! I just remembered. I buried a bone near the old oak tree. I will eat that bone.
All:	The End.

The Little Red Hen

Parts (5): Narrator, hen, pig, duck, cat

Narrator:	Once upon a time, four animals lived together on a farm.
Pig:	I am the pig. I like to spend the day in a mud puddle.
Duck:	I am the duck. The pond is the place for me!
Cat:	I am the cat. I love to sleep all day in the sun.
Little Red Hen:	And I am the Little Red Hen. I have to do *all* the work around here!!
Narrator:	One day, the Little Red Hen was looking in the yard for a bug.
Little Red Hen:	I wanted to eat it for dinner.
Narrator:	But she found a grain of wheat. It gave her an idea.
Little Red Hen:	Who will help me plant this grain of wheat?
Narrator:	She asked the pig, the duck, and the cat.
Pig:	Not I,
Narrator:	said the pig.
Duck:	Not I,
Narrator:	said the duck.
Cat:	Not I,
Narrator:	said the cat.
Little Red Hen:	Then I will do it all by myself.

Narrator:	So she did. Soon the wheat grew tall. It was ready to be cut.
Little Red Hen:	Who will help me cut the wheat and take it to be made into flour?
Narrator:	She asked the pig, the duck, and the cat.
Pig:	Not I,
Narrator:	said the pig.
Duck:	Not I,
Narrator:	said the duck.
Cat:	Not I,
Narrator:	said the cat.
Little Red Hen:	Then I will do it all by myself.
Narrator:	So she did. She came home with the flour.
Little Red Hen:	Who will help me bake the bread?
Narrator:	She asked the pig, the duck, and the cat.
Pig:	Not I,
Narrator:	said the pig.
Duck:	Not I,
Narrator:	said the duck.
Cat:	Not I,
Narrator:	said the cat.
Little Red Hen:	Then I will do it all by myself.
Narrator:	And so she did. Soon the bread was baked. It looked perfect. It smelled delicious.
Little Red Hen:	Who will help me eat this bread?
Narrator:	She asked the pig, the duck, and the cat.

Pig:	I will!
Narrator:	said the pig.
Duck:	I will!
Narrator:	said the duck.
Cat:	I will!
Narrator:	said the cat.
Little Red Hen:	Oh no you won't! I planted the wheat. I cut it down. I took it to be made into flour. I baked the bread. I will eat it all myself!
Narrator:	said the Little Red Hen. And so she did.
All:	The End.

The Three Billy Goats Gruff

Parts (6): Little Billy Goat Gruff, Middle-Sized Billy Goat Gruff, Big Billy Goat Gruff, Narrator, troll, bridge

Narrator: Welcome to our show. Our play is "The Three Billy Goats Gruff."

Narrator: Little Billy Goat Gruff saw a rickety, old bridge. On the other side of the bridge was a meadow with green, green grass and apple trees.

Little BGG: I'm the littlest billy goat. I have two big brothers. I want to go across this bridge to eat some green, green grass and apples so that I can be big like my two brothers.

Narrator: Little Billy Goat Gruff started across the bridge.

Bridge: Trip, trap, trip, trap, trip, trap.

Narrator: Just as Little Billy Goat Gruff came to the middle of the bridge, an old troll popped up from underneath.

Troll: Who is walking on my bridge?

Little BGG: It's only me, Little Billy Goat Gruff.

Troll: I'm a big, bad troll, and you are on *my* bridge. I'm going to eat you for my lunch.

Little BGG: I just want to eat some green, green grass and apples in the meadow. Please don't eat me. I'm so little. Wait until my brother comes along. He is much bigger.

Troll: All right. I guess I will. Go ahead. You can cross the bridge.

Little BGG: Thank you very much, you ugly old troll.

Troll:	What did you call me? Come back here!
Little BGG:	Bye!
Bridge:	Trip, trap, trip, trap, trip, trap.
Narrator:	Little Billy Goat Gruff ran across the bridge. He ate the green, green grass and apples. The troll went back under his bridge and went to sleep.
Narrator:	Before long Middle-Sized Billy Goat Gruff walked up to the rickety, old bridge. He too saw the meadow with the green, green grass and apple trees.
Middle BGG:	I'm the middle-sized billy goat. I have a big brother and a little brother. I want to go across this bridge to eat some green, green grass and apples so that I can be big like my big brother.
Narrator:	Middle-Sized Billy Goat Gruff started across the bridge.
Bridge:	[Louder, as Middle BGG is bigger] Trip, trap, trip, trap, trip, trap.
Narrator:	Just as the Middle-Sized Billy Goat Gruff came to the middle of the bridge, the old troll popped up again.
Troll:	Who is that walking on my bridge?
Middle BGG:	It is I, Middle-Sized Billy Goat Gruff.
Troll:	I'm a big, bad troll. You are on *my* bridge. I'm going to eat you for my lunch.
Middle BGG:	I just want to eat some green, green grass and apples in the meadow. Please don't eat me. I'm just a middle-sized billy goat. Wait until my big brother comes along. He is much bigger than I am.

Troll:	I guess I will. Go ahead and cross the bridge.
Middle BGG:	Thank you very much, you great big, ugly troll.
Troll:	What did you call me? Hey, come back here!
Middle BGG:	Oh, nothing. Bye!
Bridge:	Trip, trap, trip, trap, trip, trap.
Narrator:	Middle-Sized Billy Goat Gruff ran across the bridge. He ate the green, green grass and apples. The troll went back under his bridge and once again fell fast sleep.
Narrator:	After a while, Big Billy Goat Gruff saw the rickety, old bridge. He looked across to see the meadow with green, green grass and apple trees.
Big BGG:	I'm the biggest billy goat. I have two brothers. I want to go across this bridge to eat some green, green grass and apples just as they did.
Narrator:	So Big Billy Goat Gruff started across the bridge.
Bridge:	[Even louder this time] Trip, trap, trip, trap, trip, trap.
Narrator:	Just as Big Billy Goat Gruff got to the middle of the bridge, there was the old troll again!
Troll:	Who is that walking on my bridge?
Big BGG:	It is I, Big Billy Goat Gruff.
Troll:	I'm a big, bad troll. You are on *my* bridge. I'm going to eat you for my lunch.
Big BGG:	Really? [smiles at audience] Well, come right on up here and have a feast then. [Again grins at audience]

Narrator:	The troll climbed onto the bridge. Big Billy Goat Gruff lowered his head and charged the troll! Big Billy Goat Gruff knocked the troll clean off the bridge!
Big BGG:	Brothers, that ugly old bully won't bother us again. I've done my job and from now on we can come and go in peace. Now, I'm going to go and eat some of that green, green grass and some apples.
Bridge:	Trip, trap, trip, trap, trip, trap.
Narrator:	Big Billy Goat Gruff crossed the bridge and joined his brothers. He ate the green, green grass and apples. That mean, ugly, old troll never came back to the bridge. He learned that being mean never pays.

The Tortoise and the Hare

Parts (3): Narrator, Tortoise, Hare

Narrator: Once upon a time, a tortoise and a hare were friends.

Tortoise: I am little like a turtle. I'm slow, but I get where I'm going.

Hare: I am a rabbit. I'm fast!! Do you want to see me run?

Narrator: The friends needed some exercise. They decided to have a race.

Hare: I will beat you in this race! I can run so much faster than you can.

Tortoise: We will see about that. You are a fast runner, but I am also good at some things.

Narrator: When the race started, the hare took off at top speed.

Hare: WOO HOO!! Look at me!! I can really run!

Narrator: The tortoise took off when the race started too. She plodded along.

Tortoise: I'm slow, but I get where I'm going.

Narrator: When the race was half over, the hare was way out in front.

Hare: I can't even see Tortoise. I am so fast! I have plenty of time. I think I will take a nap.

Narrator: And so he did. He got off the path, found a soft pile of leaves, and was soon sound asleep.

Hare: ZZZZZZZZZZZ [snoring noises]

Narrator: Meanwhile, the tortoise kept plodding along.

Tortoise: I'm slow, but I get where I'm going.

Narrator: By and by, the tortoise saw the hare sleeping in the pile of leaves.

Hare: ZZZZZZZZZZZZ [snoring noises]

Tortoise: What's up with that? Oh well. I guess he knows what he is doing. I will just keep moving along.

Narrator: And so she did. She plodded and plodded. And soon, she crossed the finish line. She won the race!

Tortoise: I'm slow, but I get where I am going.

Narrator: When the hare woke up from his nap, he sped to the finish line. He was surprised to see that Tortoise was already there.

Hare: How did you do that? I run so much faster than you do.

Tortoise: Well, you know what they say: Slow and steady wins the race.

Casey at the Bat

Ernest L. Thayer (1888)

Parts (4)

1: The outlook wasn't brilliant for the Mudville nine that day.

2: The score stood four to two, with but one inning more to play,

3: And then when Cooney died at first, and Barrows did the same,

4: A pall-like silence fell upon the patrons of the game.

1: A straggling few got up to go in deep despair. The rest

2: Clung to that hope, which springs eternal in the human breast;

3: They thought, "If only Casey could but get a whack at that—

4: We'd put up even money now, with Casey at the bat."

1: But Flynn preceded Casey, as did also Jimmy Blake,

2: And the former was hoodoo, while the latter was a cake;

3: So upon that stricken multitude grim melancholy sat,

4: For there seemed but little chance of Casey getting to the bat.

1: But Flynn let drive a single, to the wonderment of all,

2: And Blake, the much despise-ed, tore the cover off the ball;

3: And when the dust had lifted, and men saw what had occurred,

4: There was Jimmy safe at second and Flynn a-hugging third.

1: Then from five thousand throats and more there rose a lusty yell;

2-3: It rumbled through the valley, it rattled in the dell;

2,3,4: It pounded on the mountain and recoiled upon the flat,

All: For Casey, mighty Casey, was advancing to the bat.

1: There was ease in Casey's manner as he stepped into his place;

2: There was pride in Casey's bearing and a smile lit Casey's face.

3: And when, responding to the cheers, he lightly doffed his hat,

4: No stranger in the crowd could doubt 'twas Casey at the bat.

1: Ten thousand eyes were on him as he rubbed his hands with dirt;

2: Five thousand tongues applauded when he wiped them on his shirt;

3:   Then, while the writhing pitcher ground the ball into his hip,

4:   Defiance flashed in Casey's eye, a sneer curled Casey's lip.

1:   And now the leather-covered sphere came hurtling through the air,

2:   And Casey stood a-watching it in haughty grandeur there.

3:   Close by the sturdy batsman the ball unheeded sped—

4:   "That ain't my style," said Casey.

ALL: "Strike one!"

1:   the umpire said.

2:   From the benches, black with people, there went up a muffled roar,

3:   Like the beating of the storm-waves on stern and distant shore;

ALL: "Kill him! Kill the umpire!"

4:   shouted some one on the stand;

1:   And it's likely they'd have killed him had not Casey raised his hand.

2:   With a smile of Christian charity great Casey's visage shone;

3:   He stilled the rising tumult; he bade the game go on;

4:   He signaled to the pitcher, and once more the dun sphere flew;

1: But Casey still ignored it, and the umpire said,

ALL: "Strike two!"

2: "Fraud!" cried the maddened thousand, and echo answered "Fraud!"

3: But one scornful look from Casey and the audience was awed.

4: They saw his face grow stern and cold; they saw his muscles strain,

1: And they knew that Casey wouldn't let that ball go by again.

2: The sneer has fled from Casey's lip, his teeth are clenched in hate;

3: He pounds with cruel violence his bat upon the plate.

4: And now the pitcher holds the ball, and now he lets it go,

1: And now the air is shattered by the force of Casey's blow.

2: Oh, somewhere in this favored land the sun is shining bright;

3: The band is playing somewhere, and somewhere hearts are light,

4: And somewhere men are laughing, and little children shout;

ALL: But there is no joy in Mudville—mighty Casey has struck out.

Book Club Ideas

Book Club

Throughout the book, you have seen icons indicating activities or discussion points that lend themselves to book club conversations. We hope you and your colleagues will take advantage of these opportunities. Our experience has taught us that learning from and with each other is a powerful way to promote innovation. In this appendix, we provide additional questions and ideas for discussion. They are organized according to the chapters in the book.

Introduction: Fluency

- Look more closely at the fluency chapter in the report of the National Reading Panel. Make notes about key insights and the classroom implications of these insights. Share these with colleagues. (The report is available at www.nationalreadingpanel .org. A shorter version of the report is available at www.nifl.gov/ partnershipforreading/publications/PFRbookletBW.pdf.)

- Select a piece of follow-up reading from the NRP website or at the National Institute for Literacy (http://nifl.gov). Make notes and share these with your colleagues.

- Think back to the beginning of your teaching career. What were you taught about teaching fluency? Share these insights with colleagues and together attempt to determine why fluency was ignored for such a long time.

Chapter 1: Fluency: What Does Research Tell Us?

- Make notes about the relationship between fluency and reading achievement. With your colleagues, write a paragraph that explains this relationship.
- Sketch and label the "bridge" metaphor.
- Use the results of the first two activities to make notes about how you can explain fluency to children.
- Talk with colleagues about what may account for children's fluency difficulties. For each reason you can identify, make instructional plans for addressing it.
- Talk with colleagues about how you can draw attention to fluency during teacher read-alouds.
- Talk with colleagues about the strengths and weaknesses of the several types of assisted reading described in the chapter.
- Brainstorm with colleagues about audiences for children's reading. Make concrete plans to begin taking advantage of these audiences.

Chapter 2: Instructional Strategies for Fluency Development

- Decide on the two or three instructional activities best suited for your classroom. Explain to your colleagues why each activity is a good fit.
- For each activity selected, make plans for implementation. Keep track of questions. Share your plans with colleagues and discuss the questions.
- For each activity selected, make plans to assess impact. That is, how will you determine if these new activities are enhancing your students' fluency? Share your ideas with colleagues and invite them to offer feedback.
- If you are currently using a commercial fluency program, evaluate it using the questions posed at the end of the chapter. If your evaluation identifies weaknesses, discuss these with your colleagues. Make plans to strengthen these weak areas if possible.

Chapter 3: Assessing Fluency Development

- Discuss each "big idea" about assessment in more detail. Decide if you agree or disagree with each, why, and what implications the ideas have for your classroom assessment plans for fluency.

- List all possible revisions to your classroom assessment plans for fluency. Then rank-order these. Explain your reasoning to your colleagues.

- For the most important revision idea from the activity above, develop an implementation plan. Share this with your colleagues and seek their feedback.

Chapter 4: Beyond Strategies

- Discuss advantages and disadvantages of having ELL students practice and perform texts written in their first languages.

- Search the web for texts written in languages your ELL students speak. Share these with your colleague.

- Develop detailed notes about the following: How will you explain fluency to parents? How will you help parents see the role they play in promoting their children's fluency?

Notes

As you work through the book, you may want to make notes here about important ideas gleaned from discussions. You can keep track of additional resources. You may also want to use these pages to reflect on changes you made in your fluency instruction and to make notes about next steps.

General Issues and Ideas

Notes

Instructional Plans

Assessment Plans

Working with ELLs

Working with Home Partners

Notes

References

Allington, R. L. (1983). Fluency: The neglected reading goal. *The Reading Teacher, 36,* 556–561.

Burgess, S. (1999). The influence of speech perception, oral language ability, the home literacy environment, and prereading knowledge on the growth of phonological sensitivity: A 1-year longitudinal study. *Reading Research Quarterly, 34,* 400–402.

Carbo, M. (1978a). Teaching reading with talking books. *The Reading Teacher, 32,* 267–273.

Carbo, M. (1978b). A word imprinting technique for children with severe memory disorders. *Teaching Exceptional Children, 11,* 3–5.

Carbo, M. (1981). Making books talk to children. *The Reading Teacher, 35,* 186–189.

Chard, D. J., Vaughn, S., & Tyler, B. (2002). A synthesis of research on effective interventions for building fluency with elementary students with learning disabilities. *Journal of Learning Disabilities, 35,* 386–406.

Chomsky, C. (1976). After decoding: What? *Language Arts, 53,* 288–296.

Cooter, R., Marrin, P., & Mills-House, E. (1999). Family and community involvement: The bedrock of reading success. *The Reading Teacher, 52,* 891–896.

Darling-Hammond, L., & McLaughlin, M. W. (1995). Policies that support professional development in an era of reform. *Phi Delta Kappan, 76,* 597–604.

Dowhower, S. L. (1987). Effects of repeated reading on second-grade transitional readers' fluency and comprehension. *Reading Research Quarterly, 22,* 389–407.

Dowhower, S. L. (1994). Repeated reading revisited: Research into practice. *Reading and Writing Quarterly, 10,* 343–358.

Eldredge, J. L. (1990). Increasing reading performance of poor readers in the third grade by using a group assisted strategy. *Journal of Educational Research, 84,* 69–77.

Eldredge, J. L., & Butterfield, D. D. (1986). Alternatives to traditional reading instruction. *The Reading Teacher, 40,* 32–37.

Eldredge, J. L., & Quinn, W. (1988). Increasing reading performance of low-achieving second graders by using dyad reading groups. *Journal of Educational Research, 82,* 40–46.

Fitzgerald, J., & Graves, M. (2004). *Scaffolding reading experiences for English language learners.* Norwood, MA: Christopher Gordon.

Hasbrouck, J., & Tindal, G. (1992). Curriculum-based oral reading fluency norms for students in grades 2 through 5. *Teaching Exceptional Children, 24*(3), 41–44.

Herman, P. A. (1985). The effect of repeated readings on reading rate, speech pauses, and word recognition accuracy. *Reading Research Quarterly, 20,* 553–564.

Howe, K., & Shinn, M. (2001). *Standard reading assessment passages (RAPS) for use in general outcome measurements: A manual describing development and technical features.* Eden Prairie, MN: Edformations.

Koskinen, P. S., & Blum, I. H. (1984). Repeated oral reading and acquisition of fluency. In J. A. Niles & L. A. Harris (Eds.), *Changing perspectives on research in reading/language processing and instruction.* Thirty-Third Yearbook of the National Reading Conference (pp. 183–187). Rochester, NY: National Reading Conference.

Koskinen, P. S., & Blum, I. H. (1986). Paired repeated reading: A classroom strategy for developing fluent reading. *The Reading Teacher, 40,* 70–75.

Kuhn, M. R., & Stahl, S. A. (2000). *Fluency: A review of developmental and remedial practices* (CIERA Rep. No. 2-008). Ann Arbor, MI: Center for the Improvement of Early Reading Achievement.

LaBerge, D., & Samuels, S. A. (1974). Toward a theory of automatic information processing in reading. *Cognitive Psychology, 6,* 293–323.

Martinez, M., Roser, N., & Strecker, S. (1999). "I never thought I could be a star": A Readers' Theatre ticket to reading fluency. *The Reading Teacher, 52,* 326–334.

McTighe, J., & Wiggins, G. (2004). *Understanding by design.* Alexandria, VA: Association for Supervision and Curriculum Development.

Mraz, M., Gruhler, D., Padak, N., Peck, J., Kinner, J., McKeon, C., & Newton, E. (2001). Questions parents ask: The FAQ project. In W. Linek, E. Sturtevant, J. Dugan, & P. Linder (Eds.), *Celebrating the voices of literacy* (pp. 252–262). Readyville, TN: College Reading Association.

National Reading Panel. (2000). *Report of the National Reading Panel: Teaching children to read. Report of the subgroups.* Washington, DC: U.S. Department of Health and Human Services, National Institutes of Health.

Padak, N., & Rasinski, T. (2004a). Fast Start: A promising practice for family literacy programs. *Family Literacy Forum, 3*(2), 3–9.

Padak, N., & Rasinski, T. (2004b). Fast Start: Successful literacy instruction that connects homes and schools. In J. Dugan, P. Linder, M. B. Sampson, B. Brarcato, & L. Elish-Piper (Eds.), *Celebrating the power of literacy, 2004. College Reading Association Yearbook* (pp. 11–23). Logan, UT: College Reading Association.

Padak, N., & Rasinski, T. (2005). *Fast Start for early readers.* New York: Scholastic.

Pinnell, G. S., Pikulski, J., Wixson, K., Campbell, J., Gough, P., & Beatty, A. (1995). *Listening to children read aloud.* Washington, DC: US Department of Education, Office of Educational Research and Improvement.

Pluck, M. (1995). Rainbow Reading programme: Using taped stories. *Reading Forum, 1*, 25–29.

Rasinski, T. V. (1995). Fast Start: A parental involvement reading program for primary grade students. In W. Linek & E. Sturtevant (Eds.), *Generations of literacy.* Seventeenth Yearbook of the College Reading Association (pp. 301–312). Harrisonburg, VA: College Reading Association.

Rasinski, T. V. (2003). *The fluent reader: Oral reading strategies for building word recognition, fluency, and comprehension.* New York: Scholastic.

Rasinski, T. V., & Hoffman, T. V. (2003). Theory and research into practice: Oral reading in the school literacy curriculum. *Reading Research Quarterly, 38*, 510–522.

Rasinski, T. V., & Padak, N. D. (1998). How elementary students referred for compensatory reading instruction perform on school-based measures of word recognition, fluency, and comprehension. *Reading Psychology: An International Quarterly, 19*, 185–216.

Rasinski, T. V., & Padak, N. (2001). *From phonics to fluency: Effective teaching of decoding and reading fluency in the elementary school.* New York: Addison-Wesley, Longman.

Rasinski, T., & Padak, N. (2004). *Effective reading strategies: Teaching children who find reading difficult* (3rd ed.). Upper Saddle River, NJ: Pearson.

Rasinski, T., & Padak, N. (2005). *Fluency first!* Chicago: The Wright Group.

Rasinski, T. V., Padak, N. D., Linek, W. L., & Sturtevant, E. (1994). Effects of fluency development on urban second-grade readers. *Journal of Educational Research, 87*, 158–165.

Renyi, J. (1998). Building learning into the teaching job. *Educational Leadership, 55*(5), 70–74.

Samuels, S. J. (1979). The method of repeated readings. *The Reading Teacher, 32*, 403–408.

Schreiber, P. A. (1991). Understanding prosody's role in reading acquisition. *Theory into Practice, 30*, 158–164.

Senechal, M., LeFevre, J., & Thomas, E. (1998). Differential effects of home literacy experiences on the development of oral and written language. *Reading Research Quarterly, 33*, 96–116.

Stahl, S., Heubach, K., & Cramond, B. (1997). *Fluency oriented reading instruction.* Athens, GA: National Reading Research Center, Universities of Maryland and Georgia.

Stevenson, B. (2002). *The efficacy of the Fast Start parent tutoring program in the development of reading skills of first grade students.* Unpublished doctoral dissertation, The Ohio State University, Columbus.

Stevenson, B., Rasinski, T., & Padak, N. (2006). Teaching fluency (and decoding) through Fast Start. In T. Rasinski, C. Blachowicz, & K. Lems (Eds.), *Teaching reading fluency* (pp. 253–264). New York: Guilford.

Taylor, E., & Collins, V. (2003). *Literacy leadership for grades 5–12.* Alexandria, VA: Association for Supervision and Curriculum Development.

Tierney, R. (1998). Literacy assessment reform: Shifting beliefs, principled possibilities, and emerging practices. *The Reading Teacher, 51,* 374–390.

Topping, K. (1987a). Paired reading: A powerful technique for parent use. *The Reading Teacher, 40,* 604–614.

Topping, K. (1987b). Peer tutored paired reading: Outcome data from ten projects. *Educational Psychology, 7,* 133–145.

Topping, K. (1989). Peer tutoring and paired reading. Combining two powerful techniques. *The Reading Teacher, 42,* 488–494.

Topping, K. (1995). *Paired reading, spelling, and writing.* New York: Cassell.

Wenglinsky, H. (2000). *How teaching matters: Bringing the classroom back into discussions of teacher quality.* Princeton, NJ: Educational Testing Service.

West, K. (1998). Noticing and responding to learners: Literacy evaluation and instruction in the primary grades. *The Reading Teacher, 51,* 550–559.